I love to learn from people who are wil~~~~ ~~ ~~~ God pull back the curtain from their lives and reveal His O'Dell Stanley does that and invites u right-side-up/upside-down view.

STASI ELDREDGE
New York Times bestselling author of *Ca*

Like the books of Anne Lamott, so full of honest and soulful searching, Kelly O'Dell Stanley's *Praying Upside Down* takes as its launchpad the precepts of the Christian faith. But what is offered here can apply to anyone, regardless of their faith—or lack thereof. What this book does is offer ways to learn and practice a humble kind of self-inventory, leading to forgiveness and generosity toward others as well as toward oneself. I found Kelly's spiritual journey compelling and her voice clear, engaging, and irresistible.

ELIZABETH BERG
Author of *The Handmaid and the Carpenter* and *The Dream Lover*

In her book, *Praying Upside Down*, Kelly O'Dell Stanley brings something entirely new for the soul to consider: What can the elements of art teach us about faith, prayer, and God? Through personal stories on family, grief, and vocation, Kelly doesn't introduce a new kind of praying as much as *a new kind of seeing*, which is what my faith really needs. This is unlike any book on prayer I've ever read.

EMILY P. FREEMAN
Author of *A Million Little Ways*

It requires no spiritual sensitivity to see God at work in a miracle, but to see God work in the everyday circumstances of our lives is another matter. *Praying Upside Down* gives us eyes to see and ears to hear the Divine Presence in the ordinariness of life. A spiritual primer on practicing the presence of God.

PHILIP GULLEY
Quaker pastor and author

In *Praying Upside Down*, Kelly O'Dell Stanley offers us a fresh perspective on not only our prayers, but also the God who answers them. Art has a way of moving and stretching us. Of making us consider our experiences in a new light. Stanley utilizes her firsthand knowledge of the artistic process to shine new truth on what it means to commune with God and the full spectrum of ways we can see His answers manifest in our lives, if our eyes are open. *Praying Upside Down* will rejuvenate any prayer life, and I believe this work is truly a gift to the Body of Christ.

SARAH KOVAC
Author of *In Capable Arms*

As a person who has always struggled with prayer, I am so grateful for Kelly O'Dell Stanley's fresh perspective, honest confessions, and grace-filled invitations. Prayer as a kind of art? What a beautiful concept.

ADDIE ZIERMAN
Author of *When We Were on Fire*

Kelly does an amazing job in *Praying Upside Down* of drawing from her rich background in graphic design and art to offer the reader fresh perspectives on an intimate relationship with God . . . perspectives that will, I believe, make us want to pray. Each chapter is wrapped around personal stories from her own pilgrimage in prayer that demonstrate great vulnerability in asking the hard questions and will inspire confidence in the God who is always with us. Each chapter ends with very practical advice that will add vitality to and increase faith for our communion with God. I had to set the book down on several occasions and marvel at the wonder of a God who offers immediate access for us all, in every circumstance of life, and welcomes us into an intimate and dynamic relationship through Christ Jesus.

DR. ALEC E. ROWLANDS
Senior pastor, Westgate Chapel, Edmonds, WA; president, Church Awakening; and author of *The Presence*

This book is CPR for your prayer life. Kelly's upside-down approach to prayer is—in all the best ways—right-side up, by pointing you straight to our sovereign God. This book will help you unleash the power of heaven in a fresh, joyful, invigorating new way.

JENNIFER DUKES LEE
Author of *Love Idol*

This book is an invitation to pray so much more richly in so many new ways. Kelly O'Dell Stanley expands our horizons about conversing with God not with more instructions but through one experience after another. If you are an artist-type, you will quickly find that she speaks your language. Even if you do not consider yourself an artist, you will be opened up to the Master Artist's point of view, which, in Kelly's words "is quite a view!"

TIMOTHY R. BOTTS
Calligrapher and author of *Doorposts*

Prayer. It can seem so . . . burdensome, time-consuming, one-sided, and complicated with all those flowery, eloquent words that we think should be the launching pad in our conversations with God. So, we choose not to pray, going through our days mute to the One who desires to, not only hear from us, but also speak to us. But in her book, *Praying Upside Down*, Kelly O'Dell Stanley takes us by the hand and challenges and equips us to see prayer from a whole new perspective, erasing what we thought prayer to be and painting a beautiful picture of what it's meant to be.

JENIFER JERNIGAN
Bible teacher and author of *Dive Deeper*

Praying Upside Down offers an invaluable antidote to the prayer life that has gone stale. We can forget the one-dimensional prayers we have been praying before bedtime all these years. Kelly O'Dell Stanley literally turns prayer on its head, transforming it into a fresh, vibrant act of creativity that refreshes the spirit. Take Kelly at her word, and you will never look at prayer the same way again.

MATT APPLING
Teacher, pastor, and author of *Life after Art* and *Plus or Minus*

PRAYING UPSIDE DOWN

A creative

prayer experience

to transform

your time

with God

KELLY O'DELL STANLEY

TYNDALE®
MOMENTUM

An Imprint of
Tyndale House Publishers, Inc.

Visit Tyndale online at www.tyndale.com.

Visit Tyndale Momentum online at www.tyndalemomentum.com.

TYNDALE, Tyndale Momentum, and the Tyndale Momentum logo are registered trademarks of Tyndale House Publishers, Inc. Tyndale Momentum is an imprint of Tyndale House Publishers, Inc.

Praying Upside Down: A Creative Prayer Experience to Transform Your Time with God

For interior art, see More about the Images on p. 261.

Designed by Nicole Grimes

Edited by Bonne Steffen

Published in association with the literary agency of The Blythe Daniel Agency, P.O. Box 64197, Colorado Springs, CO 80962-4197.

Unless otherwise indicated, all Scripture quotations are taken from the *Holy Bible*, New Living Translation, copyright © 1996, 2004, 2007, 2013 by Tyndale House Foundation. Used by permission of Tyndale House Publishers, Inc., Carol Stream, Illinois 60188. All rights reserved.

Scripture quotations marked KJV are taken from the *Holy Bible*, King James Version.

Scripture quotations marked *The Message* are taken from *The Message* by Eugene H. Peterson, copyright © 1993, 1994, 1995, 1996, 2000, 2001, 2002. Used by permission of NavPress Publishing Group. All rights reserved.

Scripture quotations marked NIV are taken from the Holy Bible, *New International Version,*® *NIV.*® Copyright © 1973, 1978, 1984, 2011 by Biblica, Inc.® Used by permission. All rights reserved worldwide.

Some people's names have been changed to protect their identities.

Library of Congress Cataloging-in-Publication Data

Stanley, Kelly O'Dell.
  Praying upside down : a creative prayer experience to transform your time with God / Kelly O'Dell Stanley.
    pages cm
  Includes bibliographical references.
  ISBN 978-1-4143-8983-7 (sc)
  1. Prayer—Christianity. I. Title.
  BV210.3.S7665 2015
  248.3'2—dc23   2014046928

Printed in the United States of America

21   20   19   18   17   16   15
 7   6   5   4   3   2   1

Dedication

For my mom, who would have been so very proud.

And for my dad, who still is.

Contents

Portrait of Igor Stravinsky *by Pablo Picasso turned upside down,*
as it was used in Betty Edwards's drawing experiment.

PRAYING UPSIDE DOWN

The real voyage of discovery consists not in seeking
new landscapes but in having new eyes.

MARCEL PROUST

I like to pray upside down.

Praying upside down doesn't involve swinging from your knees on a jungle gym. It doesn't require an inversion table or a bungee harness. In fact, it's much scarier: It's all about asking God to let you see. Truly *see*. To see Him at work, see Him in action, and let go of expectations. It might mean He'll throw your world out of orbit, turn your thoughts topsy-turvy, and change you from the inside out. It will *definitely* mean your perspective will never be the same again.

Through the years, my prayer life has run the gamut, starting with a checklist written on graph paper when I was fourteen, carefully including every item mentioned by my Sunday school teachers, camp counselors, and grandparents.

Tell God "good night" just like you do your parents. Say the Lord's Prayer every single day.

I recited prayers of penance when I entered the Catholic church in my early twenties. I offered wordless prayers of humble thanksgiving when I held my newborn children. I've raised my hands in praise and jubilation. I've sobbed on the floor in an empty church, too distraught to form coherent words. I've prayed silently on my knees, alone at home, and I've prayed out loud, in a jumble of voices as the whole congregation gathered at the altar of my church. I pray by using other people's words and I pray with my own.

But my favorite way to pray is upside down.

✳ ✳ ✳

Before you can pray upside down you have to learn to *see* upside down—or sideways or backwards, from other angles and vantage points. This discipline trains your mind to examine things from a new perspective, much as an artist does, to see what is really before you.

As an art major in college, I learned that you'll achieve better, more accurate results when you turn the image you're copying upside down. This phenomenon was first noticed by an art teacher in California named Betty Edwards. Frustrated that her drawing students couldn't recreate what she put in front of them, she impulsively turned a Picasso drawing upside down and asked them to copy it. They did—successfully.

Separate research being done at that time on left-brain/right-brain theory explained what Betty discovered in her own research. When you and I look at something, the right side of our brains identifies what we see, names the object, and makes assumptions about it based on our years of experience and observation. We might notice that one woman has a larger nose than normal or that a man's hairline is receding. But if we were asked to draw that person, we'd reach into the catalogs in the archives of our brains, pulling up a cartoonlike outline based on our general knowledge of human appearance.

As Betty Edwards explains in *Drawing on the Right Side of the Brain*, the revolutionary book she published in 1979 about this concept, turning an object upside down changes everything. When we literally flip the image on its head, our brains shift out of right-brain (or language) mode into left-brain (or visual-perceptive) mode. This changes an object from familiar to unfamiliar. Minus the advantage of assigning a top, bottom, and sides in their normal orientations, our brains no longer name or quantify the image. Preconceived ideas are discarded, which allows our brains to "see" the actual shapes that we might have missed when the image was right-side up. This is why doctors sometimes read X-rays upside down: Abnormalities are more apparent when the anatomy is oriented at a different angle.

Whatever we're viewing, once it's inverted, we become more aware of its nuances—the shapes of the dark shadows, the space between the edge of the object and the side of the page. *We see it for what it is.* The goal of reproducing the image hasn't changed, but the end result of the upside-down drawing is more accurate. We just have to try this unusual method to get there.

I was always intrigued by this idea, but it wasn't until God flipped my prayers upside down that I began to apply this concept spiritually. When my husband, Tim, and I owned two houses for two years because we couldn't sell the first one, I prayed for the woman who would buy it, whoever she was. As God seemed to open one door after another for us with the new house, but didn't provide a buyer for the old, my faith plummeted in proportion to the skyrocketing bills. Until I prayed for her—the future buyer—not me. I asked God to let me be a part of what He was doing, believing there was more at stake than my immediate financial needs.

When the house finally sold and I had processed what happened, I saw that God did amazing things during that topsy-turvy time. In spite of the frustration and uncertainty I felt, as I trusted God and let go of my worries, I discovered peace.

Some people talk about a single defining moment. My "moment" lasted for two years, but it permanently transformed the way I saw God and prayer. If you will begin to pray in the ways shown in the chapters to come, I believe these ideas will change the way you treat prayer and approach God. You will learn to notice answers you might have missed before. You will be surprised by His presence and participation in your daily life. And as you see evidence of His active role in your life, you will trust Him like you never have before.

Walk with me as I tell you my stories. We'll explore other artistic ideas too—things like white space, perspective, sketching, and more—and see how they relate to prayer. The Prayer Palette at the end of each chapter offers practical ways to implement each idea.

They're yours to use however you will. Don't feel you have to follow them to the letter. They're guidelines, not rules, to help steer you down a new path of exploration.

As we start walking, prepare to let go of your traditional compass that points left, right, or straight. Because if there's one thing I've learned about inviting God to be part of my journey, it's that "upside down" is a valid direction, although it's both unexpected and exciting. And it's one of God's favorite directions to go.

Juggling two houses at once was not my definition of fun.

CHAPTER 1

MY FIRST
UPSIDE-DOWN PRAYERS

---

*Creativity comes from looking for the unexpected
and stepping outside your own experience.*

MASARU IBUKA

When my husband and I put our house on the market, we'd never heard the term *upside down* applied to real estate. To tell the truth, it wouldn't have changed a thing if we had.

We hadn't planned to move. The house we were living in was built in 1837 and was one of the oldest homes in our town. Perched on a prime corner, it was elegantly designed with twelve-foot ceilings and crown molding. Windows stretched nearly floor to ceiling with the original wavy glass. A curved walnut banister beautifully accentuated the staircase. Our family had grown in the nine years we'd been there, and the five of us, along with my home-based business, no longer fit well in the three-bedroom house. But the rooms were large, and we weren't unhappy there. Besides, we didn't have the time, money, or energy to undertake a move. We'd made a conscious decision to stay put indefinitely.

My sister, Kerry, her husband, Doug, and their kids, Reilly and Luke, lived around the corner from us in a historic brick house (also built in 1837). One day I walked into Kerry's kitchen and she said, "Hey! My neighbor just put her house on the market. Got a minute? I want you to see it."

"Sure. But we're not going to move."

"I know that," Kerry replied. "But I think you'll like this house. Just take a look."

Looking from the outside, I wasn't all that impressed by the pale mint-green siding. When the owner gave Kerry permission to take me through the house, I didn't think the house was all that pretty on the inside, either. June, a widow in her eighties, had been in the house for thirty years. When she and her husband had moved in, they put their own decorating touches on the house but didn't update again after that. Drab, quaint pastoral scenes covered the faded, golden wallpapers. Sculpted shag carpet, also gold, filled the living room. Everything else was painted mint green. *They must have bought an industrial-sized tub of it,* I thought as I imagined the colors I would choose to cover that prolific pastel. As a graphic designer, I couldn't look at a home without mentally redecorating.

In the dining room and bedrooms, you could see the hardwood floors. *Yes!* Busy patterns consumed the walls, yet if you stood back and squinted just so, you could see the classic (though somewhat crooked) lines of the doors and multipaned transom windows. Eleven-foot ceilings. Built-in bookcases. Brick fireplace with a wooden mantel hiding behind an ugly striped couch.

With my love for old homes and my creative streak, I started to get excited. This house could be arty and eclectic and comfy and just right for our family. It was perfect.

That is, if we were going to move—which we weren't.

This decision was reinforced when we walked into the kitchen with its acoustic tile ceiling, homemade cabinets, yellow Formica countertops, and gray paneling. Not to mention the strange placement of the appliances (stove next to sink, conspicuously absent dishwasher). On to the bathroom: No amount of bubble bath could convince me to take a bath in there. Den: not bad if you like a faded golf trophy pattern adorning your curtains, dark fake wood paneling, and a dirty mottled brown shag carpet. The big front room with a separate entrance would make a great office, but the former efficiency apartment was painted the familiar mint green with indoor/outdoor teal carpet, a kitchenette that might have been cute under the grime, and a stall shower. Upstairs, the rooms weren't so bad—plain, a little drab, more shag carpet (orange, this time).

But by the end of that walk through, I'd forgotten that we didn't want to move. I was hooked. Although I saw the flaws and all the time and energy this house would need, I also saw promise. I could picture our family there. *Maybe we could make it work.*

So Kerry and I dragged Tim, my resident handyman, over for

his opinion. He quickly pointed out the exposed wiring, crooked plaster walls, and leaky windows. Tim exhaled his signature sigh, knowing he would have a lot of work cut out for him, but he also saw the potential. The house was a bargain. And after sixteen years of marriage, he knew when I had my heart set on something.

Although the new address needed a complete overhaul, there were definitely some strong selling points, too. Like the fact that the home shared a driveway with my sister's house, and our kids could play together in the adjoining yards. Once the renovations were complete, we'd have a great place to call home—same square footage as our current one but with more rooms, a smaller mortgage, and really great neighbors.

Next Hurdle: My Parents

My parents always believed I was capable of practically anything, but they disapproved of how many of those things I tried to squeeze into my schedule. I didn't need more chaos, commitments, or excuses to spend (more) money. So when I called Mom and Dad to come look at the house with us, I flinched in anticipation of their response. My worries were needless; they loved it and jumped right into planning mode with us.

I wanted one more person to see it—my grandmother, Mah. At ninety, she was strong, outspoken, and slow to accept change. Yet she saw that this house would make "a good family home" and offered to loan us money to buy it. "I don't want you to carry two mortgages at once," she said. "Once you sell your current home, you can pay me back."

A few weeks later, Mah amended her offer; the money was a gift, not a loan. There was just one stipulation: "Don't you *ever* borrow money against this house." Agreed.

We were giddy. The proceeds from the sale of our old house would more than cover the remodeling costs. We felt grateful—and a little embarrassed about how spoiled we were—as everything fell into place. *This has to be God*, we thought, as one door after another flew open. *God is so good to us.* We knew the economy was slowing down, but we tithed. We went to church faithfully. In our heart of hearts, we smugly believed God would take care of this for us.

It didn't matter that big old houses tended to stay on the market for a long time, or that the house we were selling had sat empty for six months before *we* bought it. We'd loved it, and so would someone else. We were excited to see how God would accomplish this sale and couldn't wait to testify about the mighty ways God had moved in our lives.

We bought the house.

Out with the Old, In with the New

My husband and I spent that summer running over to the "complex," as my mom dubbed the section of the block occupied by her two daughters. I own my own graphic design business and work from a home office, so I interrupted my work several times a day to supervise the electricians, apply another coat of paint, sand kitchen cabinets, tear out carpet, and measure for curtains. Our bodies ached from the hard work and it felt like we didn't sleep for months, but at least we didn't have to live in the middle of this construction zone, surrounded by dusty sawhorses and piles of debris. At the end of each day, we crashed in our old house—a (relatively) quiet, clean place. With three kids, our living quarters were chaotic but livable.

As wonderful as the situation was, it wasn't completely ideal. We'd had the dubious pleasure of putting our house on the market right before the housing market dropped. *Bottomed out* is more like it. Six months into the project, we were struggling. We'd spent all the money we had and were going into serious debt, too far to be comfortable. But years of faithful prayer about many things had taught me that the answers I sought were sometimes a long time coming and often required quite a bit of work on my part. It was way too soon to give up hope.

In the eight years leading up to this point, I'd drawn closer to God until He had become everything to me. I went from feeling generous when I threw twenty dollars into the offering plate, to giving larger offerings, to tithing on my net income and before long, on every single thing that came in the door. I saw God provide for the needs of my husband, our kids, and my growing business. He taught me about the power of prayer. He revealed Himself in unexpected ways. I watched as my husband moved into new roles, becoming a Sunday school teacher, children's church leader, and worship singer. We were "all in," blessed beyond measure. It was just a matter of time before God would come through for us again.

So I acted in faith, anointing the old house.[1] My friends joined me in prayer, fervently interceding on my behalf. We dabbed olive oil on doorposts and prayed that those who entered the house would feel the presence of God. We had already hired the best realtor in town, and I put my marketing skills to work. I created a sales flyer, complete with descriptive captions pointing out the best features. I even made witty yard signs to attract drive-by traffic. And yet in all those months, nothing happened. Nada.

One afternoon, I was cleaning the old house, preparing for a rare showing, only the second or third at that time. As I vacuumed the bedroom, doubts flooded my thoughts. *Lord, please let us sell*

> *Years of faithful prayer had taught me that the answers I sought were sometimes a long time coming and required work on my part. It was way too soon to give up hope.*

this house. Things are getting serious. Please. Tears trickled from the corners of my eyes. We were broke and had been charging things like we had the money to pay it all back. My largest client had recently filed bankruptcy, owing me more than $8,000 that I'd probably never see. *Lord, what are we going to do if the house doesn't sell soon? We're in deep trouble.*

Then a still, small voice—powerful yet quiet at the same time—said to me, "PRAY FOR THE WOMAN WHO WILL BUY THIS HOUSE."

It wasn't an audible voice, but it was one I recognized. The few times I'd experienced this sort of whisper, I knew I was hearing from God. The words were infused with layers of meaning that went beyond the individual words that were spoken. I turned off the vacuum and sat on the edge of my purple quilt, overwhelmed by the holiness of the moment. I soaked in the deafening stillness, newly aware that this predicament was, indeed, under His control.

So I prayed for the situations in this as-yet-unidentified woman's life to line up so that she'd be ready to buy. *Move her. Set things in motion. Prepare her. Bless her. Touch her. Be with her. Guide her. Speak to her.* I didn't know if I was praying about work (a new job or a transfer for the woman or her husband) or financial difficulties or getting pregnant or aging parents needing care or finishing a degree to get a job. All the while, though, I was thinking, *Okay, this is cool—even if it is a little bit backwards. Take the focus off me, Lord.*

That night I wrote in my journal, "Maybe I need to quit worrying about my house selling or my financial situation and pray for someone else. I can do that. She (whoever she is) needs the prayers. . . . If I have to wait, I have to wait."

Redirecting my prayers helped. I was tired of praying for myself. Tired of thinking about money. Tired of calculating and recalculating square footages and installation costs and how much we'd owe on credit cards once the house finally sold. Instead, I fell to my knees for the family that would someday fill this home with their furniture and clothes and line the historic stairway with family photos. Every time I prayed for *them*, though, I felt a correction, a little hitch: *her*, not them.

Okay, Lord, I'll pray for just her (but I kept sneaking in little blessings for her husband, because there was no way a single woman would tackle this big, high-maintenance old house on her own).

The showing the next day yielded a second one. The family who was looking at the house had narrowed it down to two finalists. I rejoiced—this must be it! But then Rusty, our realtor, called. Bad news. The family chose the other house. He was so sorry.

What is going on, Lord? I don't understand. I thought You were finally answering.

"PRAY FOR HER."

My panic eased momentarily, but I wanted *my* prayers answered too. Since I was self-employed and sometimes had to wait six to eight weeks between checks, I'd already mastered the art of juggling funds, moving money back and forth between my business and our personal checking as needed. But I wasn't able to make everything balance anymore. I was having to make choices—pay one bill or the other, but not both—and getting farther and farther behind.

Each month, when our mortgage was due, I quieted the anxiety in my gut. I wrote the check and mentally lifted it up to God. *This is my offering, Lord. This is for her. I can hold on just a little longer to help someone else.*

The rooms in the new place slowly came together as my family pitched in. Our son, Bobby, and his six-months-older cousin, Luke, sat on top of the cab of the pickup truck, examining the debris we piled into it. Dad yanked out the drop ceiling and warped wallboards of the kitchen while I steadied the ladder and ran after tools. We hung and painted crisp white wainscoting. My niece, Reilly, learned how to use a cordless screwdriver and helped attach the new hinges and handles to the cabinets that Dad and I rebuilt, sanded, and painted. In between tasks, we'd step inside Kerry and Doug's air-conditioned kitchen and gulp down some cold water. Finally our do-it-yourself projects were complete and the outside contractors came in to install new flooring, lighting, and countertops.

When I was alone, I prayed as I worked, filled with a peace I'd never felt before, a holiness in the hush of the empty house. *God, You're here in this place.* One weekend, after the carpet was installed, we carried our sleeping bags from the old house to the new one, plugged a movie into the DVD player connected to the television we'd already installed, and camped out on the living room floor. I remember giggles, microwave popcorn, and not caring that I was too old to sleep on the floor. Other than my back protesting, the night was perfect.

Eventually, the renovation was complete. Spiritually, I still had some distance to go. When my friend Vickie joined us in praying for the house to sell, she envisioned me dancing through the old house with a feather boa to celebrate the sale. So she brought me a boa, and our prayer group gathered in the vacated living room, begging God to intervene, filling the empty rooms with our pleas. I knew He would answer. But *when*? I kept trying to shove fear out of my thoughts and instead love the future buyer the way God must, since He was making the sale of my house revolve around what she needed. My heart felt simultaneously overlooked—why did this woman matter more than me?—and buoyant, because God had given me enough nudges that I believed He was working on the resolution.

I just couldn't figure out what was taking Him so long.

When our house sold, it was a reason to celebrate—and pay attention.

CHAPTER 2

THE ART OF MOVING ON

> *To make art, we have to be able to enter a complicated*
> *dance between knowing and not knowing,*
> *between what's clear and what's chaotic.*

HEATHER SELLERS

We postponed moving day as long as we could, in an effort to keep the old house furnished for potential showings. But if the new house was a gift given to us by God, why on earth wouldn't we live there? After Tim and I carried one drop-leaf walnut table down the block, trying not to curse at each other in the process, we scheduled the movers.

A friend of Kerry's offered to rent our old house, but she needed a year-long lease and a payment lower than the amount we owed the bank each month. We graciously declined and kept praying.

We applied to refinance our mortgage at a lower interest rate, but the bank saw the direction the economy was heading, and after reviewing our balance statement said, "Sorry, but no." I longed for the days when you could slam the phone down to hang up. Instead, I clicked a little button on my cell phone and tried not to cry.

We lowered the asking price again, knowing we might never get out from under this debt. Credit card companies—seeing the advantage to be gained from our disadvantage—kept raising our lines of credit as our balances neared those ceilings again and again. And they'd raise our interest rates with every payment that was a day or two late. Before long, the monthly minimum amount due exceeded our house payment.

With every new bill, the sick feeling in the pit of my stomach came back. It was my dirty little secret. My parents never had debt. My sister and her husband were careful and smart with their money. My grandparents had done very well financially, starting with nothing in the Depression and building an estate of value. I'd always spent too much. Nobody thought I could handle my money well. They were right, but I still hated Mom's questions. "No, Mom, we're doing fine. . . . Yes, we have some bills, but it's under control. Don't worry," I'd say, changing the subject as my stomach churned and sweat broke out on my forehead.

The *only* thing that kept me going was the belief that God was in this. Surely He wouldn't leave us now. We hadn't imagined His involvement. He would find a way out for us.

Or, if not for us, for that mysterious woman I had yet to meet.

Hope Raised—and Shattered

One day in the neighborhood coffee shop, a woman named Rosanne sat down with me. "Hey, I might want to look at your house sometime." Our sons were in the same class in elementary school, but Rosanne's family had just recently moved here and I didn't know her well. I'd heard murmurs that she was getting a divorce, but I didn't think she was serious about the house until Rusty said he'd scheduled a showing. We were asking well beyond her price range, but she loved the house and gave us an offer anyway.

The fleeting feeling of hope I'd had—*maybe she's the one!*—vanished as quickly as it had come. The house had originally listed at $179,000. We'd lowered it to $165,000. She offered $100,000. We said no and didn't bother to make a counteroffer. *She must not be the one we're praying for*, we declared, *because God wouldn't ask us to take such a loss.*

Over the next several months, we lowered the price again. And again. We had open houses with no visitors at all. We adored the new place, though, and tried to ignore the 3,000-square-foot thorn in our sides just around the corner.

Even though I was convinced Rosanne was not "that woman," she made another offer. A little higher, but not enough. In spite of our desperation, we couldn't accept. We knew making a profit on the house was out of the question at this point, but we would still be $7,000 shy of paying off the bank if we accepted, so we were stuck.

Our accountant called a few days later to let us know that for the first time ever, we were getting a tax refund—$6,000! The next day, Rusty called me. "Rosanne has made another offer. Less than asking price, the same as before, but she's agreed to take it 'as is,' no matter what the inspection shows. This is a gift. I think you should take it."

"Rusty, we can't. We've lost so much money. She's offering less than we paid for the house twelve years ago."

"I understand," he said, "but think about something for me. How much is your mortgage?"

"$1,000."

"And with insurance and utilities and taxes, how much is it costing you to keep that house?"

"About $2,000 a month."

"And how many months would it take to make up that $7,000 difference?"

I sighed, suddenly hating math. "Three and a half."

"You've seen the market. Do you really think this house is going to sell in less than that?" He paused. "I think you need to take it. I'll cut my commission. You'll still have to pay Rosanne's realtor's fee, but not mine."

I hung up, heartbroken but touched by Rusty's generosity. I did what I always did when I didn't know what else to do: I called my mom. As soon as she heard the latest development, she offered the extra thousand we'd need to make it work. Tim wasn't enthusiastic about the plan. "No way," he expressed initially. However, after a few hours mulling over the situation, he saw Rusty's wisdom. And with a big sigh, he said, "Okay, let's do it."

Adjusting My Expectations

I expected to be joyful but I wasn't. How could I be happy about the sale? Nothing went the way I wanted it to. And then I realized, *Wait. No, this isn't what I imagined. It's not what we* thought *we wanted. But God made a way for us to sell the house.*

The pieces quickly clicked into place. As we became acquainted, I learned that Rosanne's husband had accepted a job transfer, relocating their family from several states away. Rosanne hadn't wanted to move, but she did anyway—and then, six months later, her husband ended the marriage. They needed to sell their house before Rosanne received the divorce settlement that enabled her to make a down payment.

She'd loved our house the moment she stepped inside, enough to keep asking until it fell into her price range. With her husband gone, Rosanne needed to resurrect the career she left when her kids were born. She had to find a well-paying job so she could meet the monthly mortgage payment as well as provide for her kids. She didn't have to wait long, and her new job was within walking distance, so she could relax at home during her lunch hour.

God wasn't late. He was right on time. He saw the big picture, knew what was at stake, and steadily put things in motion. My God hadn't let me down—my expectations had been off, that's all. I'd made the erroneous assumption that since it was *my* house, and *my* prayer, it was about *me*.

> *God wasn't late. He was right on time. He saw the big picture, knew what was at stake, and steadily put things in motion. My God hadn't let me down.*

Even as my emotional side complained about how much this ordeal cost us, my brain began to put that loss in perspective. We had received an unexpected tax refund that nearly covered what we needed, then Mom volunteered the rest. And let's not forget, my grandmother had basically given us a house. Who can say that? We had loads of debt, but without a mortgage, we could repurpose that amount of money each month to pay off our bills. Tim and I had a stable marriage; three healthy, beautiful children; a loving family that was quick to offer help (whether that meant hands-on labor, financial help, or emotional support); good jobs; and a house that perfectly suited our family's needs. What in the world was I whining about?

After all, Rosanne was in a more difficult place, leaving a twenty-year marriage and reestablishing herself. We couldn't help with any of the emotional strain, but we could be part of a blessing for her by offering a physical place in which to rebuild. There were plenty of renovating projects Rosanne *could* do, but she didn't *have* to do anything before moving in. Her kids loved the colors our kids had chosen for their rooms. The Southern belle in Rosanne loved the wide front porch with a swing, which we agreed to leave for her. She fit that house better than we had, and our new home fit us. In our old house, the one filled with the prayers of my friends and family on her behalf, she would again find stability. And through this process, she got to see God answer her prayers too.

Seeing Clearly

It took two long years, but when the sold sign was hammered into my old front yard, my vision cleared, and I could see. *You've blessed both of our families, Lord.* When God asked me to pray for a woman whom I didn't know, I'd been praying upside down—backwards from the world's point of view. Instead of focusing on myself, I saw enough of God's hand to believe that He was up to something. While I was suggesting all kinds of ways for God to answer my prayer because I was worried about one thing (money), Rosanne spent that year and a half facing one new obstacle after another. Overwhelmed with the changes and exhausted by her trials, she was also struggling to see what God was doing during this season. I didn't know much about her faith, but I knew that she attended church and prayed. All that time, as she prayed and as Tim and I prayed, God kept working—toward something bigger, something better, eventually answering our prayers by answering hers, too. Getting a glimpse of God's plan was a lovely gift for both Rosanne and me.

Maybe you are feeling stuck. Worried that God doesn't hear you. Convinced that you don't deserve to have your prayers answered. Wondering how, when, or even *if* God will answer you. Your need may be huge. You may be lonely, looking for someone to spend your life with. Maybe you've lost a child, spouse, or your best friend. Perhaps you struggle with addictions or are facing bankruptcy. Maybe you have been abused. You might have been hurt by "religion" or had someone twist the words of the Bible against you. You may have seen the way God answered one of your prayers

This is your chance to give prayer another chance, or to deepen your existing practice of prayer. To ask and to watch for answers. To try to see God in a new way.

and didn't like it, so you're afraid to try praying again. Or maybe you consider yourself in a pretty good place right now and the issues you struggle with don't seem particularly extreme, but still they flood your mind, leaving little room for prayer.

We all face hurdles. Our issues, personalities, and abilities color our faith and guide our behavior. Whether you want to overcome issues from the past or you're taking your first tentative steps of faith—wherever you fall on the continuum of human experience—this is your chance to give prayer another chance, or to deepen your existing practice of prayer. To ask and to watch for answers. To try to see God in a new way.

During the two years I struggled financially, God wasn't idle. Just because I had run out of things to do didn't mean He had. I had to look at the situation upside down in order to see what was happening right in front of me.

You can too.

Upside-down and right-side-up can exist simultaneously, just as Jesus saw one way and everyone else saw another.

CHAPTER 3

JESUS TURNED THE WORLD UPSIDE DOWN

The world is wrong side up. It needs to be turned upside down in order to be right side up.

BILLY SUNDAY

Art, simply put, is a way to capture what an artist sees, to repackage that vision in a way that allows others to see the same thing. Being a Christian isn't all that different—it's repackaging our vision of Christ to allow others to see Him. And the best way to represent Him is by doing the things He did.

Throughout the Bible, Jesus surprised His followers—and critics—with His unexpected answers. As someone who grew up feeling as though I didn't fit in because I saw things differently than most, I find comfort in this. If Jesus didn't settle for the obvious or anticipated solution, we don't have to either. Because He wasn't like anyone else, we are also free to be unique. As we turn away from this world that encourages us to be just like everyone else (only skinnier, richer, and more successful), I think Jesus watches eagerly for us to break out of the mold—as He did. As long as we model our behavior on His, we can't go wrong. He showed us over and over that *His* approach is different from the world's approach.

> *Praying upside down is a way to move your prayers away from the expected so that you can learn something new, hear an answer you didn't anticipate, or see God in a unique way.*

It's worth repeating: <u>Jesus turned the world upside down</u>.

Praying upside down is a way to move your prayers away from the expected so that you can learn something new, hear an answer you didn't anticipate, or see God in a unique way. It isn't a form of manipulation or an attempt to trick God into giving you what you want. And it's not a time-consuming, difficult, lofty type of prayer. It's a set of tools that will grow and change and adapt as you use them.

✳ ✳ ✳

One Sunday morning when our son, Bobby, was six, he left the pew we were sitting in and walked straight to the front of the church, up the steps onto the platform, right in the middle of our worship time. Pastor Nathan was sitting in a chair off to the side, putting the finishing touches on his sermon notes. Bobby circled around the worship leader, ignored the musicians, and climbed into the seat next to Nathan. With a sigh, he leaned back and then scooted to the edge of the chair. The big smile and hug Nathan gave him weren't a surprise—Nathan had taught all the children that they were always welcome to come up front. That day, as I watched through tears, I finally understood the beauty of having direct access to God, knowing that He welcomes me and you with joy. No matter who's watching.

This must be what Jesus meant when He spoke to the disciples who tried to shoo the children away from Him.

> "Let the children come to me. Don't stop them! For the Kingdom of God belongs to those who are like these children. I tell you the truth, anyone who doesn't receive the Kingdom of God like a child will never enter it."
> LUKE 18:16-17

Jesus broke with convention and offered all that He had to those who had nothing. No qualifications required. No secret handshake. Through His example, He showed that all we need to approach Him is the confidence that He will not stop us.

> "Anyone who welcomes a little child like this on my behalf welcomes me, and anyone who welcomes me also welcomes my Father who sent me. Whoever is least among you is the greatest."
> LUKE 9:48

Nathan demonstrated this to me, too. When he named Tim and me as elders in our church, he kept us from feeling prideful or exalted about our new position. "In most companies," he explained, "the president is at the top and power filters from the top down. But in the church, every person matters. The pyramid is upside down, with the majority of people—those considered the 'least'—at the top."

In God's world, the blessings come from serving rather than being served. From loving rather than just being loved. From being welcomed by the Master, even if no one else thinks we belong.

✳ ✳ ✳

My mom was a high school nurse. One year she befriended a boy (I'll call him Chris) who came to see her regularly. He and his siblings didn't have much compared to the other students, and their single parent wasn't very involved in their lives. Chris was witty and bright, but he was so self-conscious about his extremely crooked teeth that he covered his mouth whenever he smiled. Without Chris's knowledge, Mom asked a local orthodontist to create an imaginary county dental fund (to which she was the sole contributor) in order to pay for his braces. Her reward? Watching Chris's self-confidence blossom.

In the Bible, the Pharisees didn't hide their good deeds but took pride in their public displays. Jesus chastised them.

> "Watch out! Don't do your good deeds publicly, to be admired by others, for you will lose the reward from your Father in heaven."
>
> MATTHEW 6:1

Jesus flip-flopped public faith for private, emphasizing that what's in a person's heart is more important than a person's actions, and reminding us that God's reward system isn't the same as this world's.

And then, to further confound the world, He declared that the strict dietary laws the people followed to ensure a place in heaven no longer mattered.

> "Can't you see that the food you put into your body
> cannot defile you? . . . It is what comes from inside that
> defiles you. For from within, out of a person's heart, come
> evil thoughts, sexual immorality, theft, murder, adultery,
> greed, wickedness, deceit, lustful desires, envy, slander,
> pride, and foolishness."
> MARK 7:18, 20-22

This was about so much more than changing the rules. It was about changing the standards by which people measured themselves and about releasing them from the judgments they brought on themselves through their actions. Jesus declared that of the Ten Commandments given to Moses, the first two are the most important—love God with all that you are, and love your neighbor as yourself. The loopholes were gone. At the same time as Jesus freed us from living up to the strict religious laws, though, the guidelines actually got harder because He cared about the motivation behind the actions too.

> "You have heard the commandment that says, 'You must
> not commit adultery. But I say, anyone who even looks at
> a woman with lust has already committed adultery with
> her in his heart.'"
> MATTHEW 5:27-28

Suddenly, it was a level playing field again. None of us can live up to God's standards, but we don't have to anymore. He took the burden off of our shoulders and took us by the hand.

Upside-Down Answers

The year I turned forty, my hairdresser concocted a perfect color blend to match the red in my hair that was being noticeably edged out. The optometrist helped me choose appropriate reading glasses. When I thought I'd pulled something in my back, nothing (including time) seemed to help until my doctor prescribed an anti-inflammatory. I'm quite skilled at avoiding housework, but when I did do it, I suddenly noticed that it hurt to bend over to pick up dirty socks off the floor. When I stooped to get pots and pans out of lower cabinets, I needed a wall or chair to pull myself back up. After sitting in my desk chair for a long stretch, my knees throbbed when I stood. And, eventually, I found I could no longer kneel at the altar at church without the resulting pain pushing all thoughts of prayer out of my mind. That's when I decided something had to be done.

I asked Mike, one of the elders at my church, to pray for me. He suggested another idea. He'd pray for my knees if I would pray for his back. A year earlier, as he stood in a yard talking to a friend, a tree literally fell on top of him. His friend's neighbor was cutting it down, and a large limb fell the wrong way and hit Mike on his shoulder and hip. After he was released from the hospital, his restless movements during church showed his discomfort. He'd sit, then stretch; pace, then wince; squat and start the process all over again. Even after Mike's stiff back brace came off, anyone could see that he was uncomfortable. My pain was nothing compared to his, but since my own prayers had grown tired and didn't seem to be effective, I was game.

Every time my knees ached, throbbed, or even twinged, I prayed for Mike's back. Whenever he felt pain in his back, he sent up a prayer for my knees. Within weeks, we weren't completely healed, but we were both better. My doctor had prescribed a new low-dose medication that worked better than the first one; Mike still walks a little stiffly at times—he experienced permanent nerve damage from the accident—but he no longer twists and fidgets to find a comfortable position, and every Sunday he jumps up the steps to take his position as a praise singer. Kneeling in worship has become sweeter to me now.

When we found a way to get unstuck, God answered. When we tried something new, we saw different results. By opening our eyes to creativity in prayer, we are asking God to open the doors of the unknown and let us see Him through them. As hard as we try, we may never see with the wisdom and clarity and compassion that God does, or anticipate the answers He provides. After all, we wouldn't have dreamed that God would

> *God is the Master of Creativity, the original Artist, and He rarely responds in the ways we expect.*

send a good man—His Son, Jesus—to pay the price for all the bad in this world. Or that Jesus would take a punishment He didn't deserve in order to free us from enduring it.

God is the Master of Creativity, the original Artist, and He rarely responds in the ways we expect. In one instance, my friend Peggy noticed her boss's crazy hours and schedule. She listened to her boss's complaints, and witnessed the stress that filled her days. In the least judgmental way possible, Peggy prayed for Susan to get her priorities straight and to find a simpler, more sane life. It worked. Susan lost the grant that funded their work, and her life immediately slowed down.

Peggy was thrilled that the Lord answered, but she wasn't antic- ipating one thing: When the grant went away, so did Peggy's job. Over time, though, she discovered the depths of wisdom in God's answer.

"Even though I was praying for Susan, God was really ordering my steps," Peggy told me. "He was putting things in place for me." Because she lost her job, she had more time to spend working on home improvements. A year later, she and Nathan sold that house, moved into a new place, and not long afterward were asked to take over the leadership of our church. When Nathan (a major in the National Guard) was called to serve for a year in Afghanistan, Peggy prayed and studied, growing into a strong and dynamic teacher. As she says now, "God takes something little—a small request—and replaces it with a much bigger answer."

God's answers to our prayers may seem upside down. He may ask you to forgive, even if you are the one who is wronged. He may ask you to become the wife your husband needs, rather than turning your husband into the man you always dreamed of. He may not save your job, but He might give you the time you've always needed to learn more about Him, or free your schedule to finish the renovations on your kitchen. He might not deliver you from poverty but instead teach you how to budget, balance, and take care of what He's provided. Or He may show you that even if you have very little, when you can find ways to give what you do have, you will feel wealthy.

Praying upside down can be a literal flip-flop of your prayers, like my prayers for Rosanne and Mike or any type of prayer that is unconventional, unexpected, or unusual. The power isn't in the asking or dependent on your ability to find a creative way to ask— it's in the creative and surprising ways in which God answers. I won't promise that you will get what you want, but you will see God in a new way. If your prayer life feels stagnant, if your words are stilted and mundane, this is a chance to try something new and challenge what you've always done.

Throughout this book, as I unpack the different tools I've discovered as an artist and show how each one applies to prayer, give yourself permission to explore. If my approach doesn't apply to your situation, but you see a way to tweak it so that it makes sense to you, then do that. If an exercise in the Prayer Palette at the end of a chapter sparks an idea that takes you in a different direction, allow yourself to try it. Creativity is about exploring. And praying upside down is about following in whatever direction God points you.

In Luke 22:42, Jesus prayed, "Father, if thou be willing, remove this cup from me: *nevertheless* not my will, but thine, be done" (KJV, emphasis added). *Nevertheless* is a powerful word you rarely hear these days. When included in prayer it means that even if nothing make sense to us yet, even if we don't know what to expect, we want the best that God has. We're acknowledging that, even two thousand years later, Jesus continues to provide a fresh approach. When we pray upside down, we're looking at our situations from a different point of view—His—and saying, "I may not always understand—*nevertheless*, I'm willing. Turn me upside down, if that's what You want."

Because if that's *His* point of view—oh, what a view that must be.

Even when he was busy, my dad always made me feel at home in his studio.

CHAPTER 4

DRAWING NEAR

*Creativity involves breaking out of established patterns
in order to look at things in a different way.*

EDWARD DE BONO

"So, has any of your dad's artistic talent rubbed off on you?"

I was standing near my dad during an opening of one of his one-man shows. The pale hardwood floor glinted in the strong spotlights illuminating his artwork. Dad's paintings of rural Midwestern landscapes hung on the bright white walls. People filled the art gallery, heads tilted to view one painting after another while they sipped their wine and waited to meet him. Mom, who would have preferred to be at home reading a book in her fleece robe rather than talking to strangers, avoided the limelight at these events. Kerry usually stayed close to her, but I liked to be with Dad. I'd leave his side only to grab another cream cheese and turkey-filled pinwheel or to look for the little red dots that meant a painting had sold, silently tallying up the total to whisper to Dad in between conversations.

As admirers stood in line to talk to Dad, these kind men and women talked to me, inevitably asking if I was an artist. Dad would pause his other conversation, touch my arm, and smile. "Yes, and she got my red hair, too."

I was always so proud to belong to him, to have so much of him inside me. But I knew I'd finally succeeded on my own merits when I was in my late twenties. Dad went to an advertising association event with me, and someone said to him, "So you're Kelly Stanley's father?" For at least that moment, Dad was defined by his relationship to me instead of the other way around.

Dad was in the advertising world long before I was, though. After graduating from the American Academy of Art in Chicago, he worked as a commercial artist doing catalog layouts. His boss, a frustrated painter himself, had seen Dad's success at weekend art fairs. Sometimes Dad would sell out before the end of the first day and would paint all night to have more art to sell on day two. "You can come back anytime you want," his boss told him. "I'll always have a job for you. But now's the time to see if you can ride this success any further."

So when I was eleven months old, we moved into a vacant house in rural Ladoga, Indiana, that had belonged to several generations of my family. Mom and Dad had enough savings to live there for one year. If he couldn't sell enough paintings to support us, we'd go back to Chicago. They loved the small community, though, and his work continued to sell. They never considered leaving.

Growing up, I spent summer weekends lying on my stomach on a blanket at outdoor art fairs, the pages of my latest Nancy Drew book reflecting sunlight into my face while Dad sold paintings, mostly to longtime repeat customers. Days when we were home, Dad would finish his bacon and eggs and head out back to his studio so he could paint without interruption, although he never seemed to mind if we'd wander in to talk to him.

The building he painted in formerly housed a summer kitchen. Now, light streamed in from a picture window next to his drawing board. From Dad's swivel stool, he could see the cornfields and trees surrounding our house. Sketch pads and large art books lined the shelves behind his workspace, and on another wall, Best of Show ribbons hung in colorful, festive rows over a crowded cutting board and framing area. One step down from that room, separated by rough wooden beams but not really enclosed, was the gallery. Sunshine from the skylight above angled across the floor. Paintings hung haphazardly on the wood-paneled walls. Dozens more, matted but not framed, were stacked on a wide wooden shelf. The room was encircled by a narrow shelf supporting an old metal train track and one of the dozens of model trains removed from the rack of trains displayed on another wall. I loved it when he'd let us turn on the transformer and the little train would clickety-clack around and around in circles.

Our house was its own private gallery, crowded with framed paintings and drawings, many obtained by an informal trade between artists at the end of a show. I spent many long afternoons, draped sideways across a chair, studying these paintings. There were acrylics, watercolors, photos, and pencil drawings. Realistic barns, doorways, and houses; fields and flowers and trees. Stained glass hung in most of our windows and handmade ceramic vessels decorated the tables and shelves.

I didn't play with Barbies, but gravitated toward Dad's typography books, silkscreen frames and linoleum blocks Mom ordered from art supply catalogs, and cameras. Even though we lived in rural Indiana, Dad's vocation brought us little glimpses of culture and art. I loved that. *Once I'm old enough to make my own decisions, I'm going to move to a big city and do something even more exciting,* I promised myself.

I knew I lacked that indefinable *something* that Dad had. I didn't feel the urge to paint or sculpt, but I spent hours tracing letters, coloring geometric designs with vibrant markers, and writing and designing newsletters and magazines for my pen pals. I wrote to my cousins, daughters of my parents' out-of-state friends, girls in Korea and China found through organizations advertising in the back of my magazines, and (in my teens) boys I met at statewide FFA camps. My cousin and I designed business cards for the "KAO Club," a group we created for people who happened to share our initials. We were the only two members, of course, and still sometimes call each other "KAO#1" and "KAO#2."

> *I spent hours tracing letters, coloring geometric designs with vibrant markers, and writing and designing newsletters and magazines for my pen pals. Looking back, it seems obvious where my aptitudes and interests lay.*

Looking back, it seems obvious where my aptitudes and interests lay. But when it came time to choose a college major, I wanted a career that I believed was more academically challenging than art, hopefully leading to a job with a steady paycheck. After attending a summer honors program in architecture at Ball State University, I set my heart on studying at Ball State's prestigious College of Architecture and Planning. This career path combined two things I loved—creativity and math—and sounded cool and challenging.

The foundational classes in the program ignited my passion for design, and as we moved from abstract design concepts to specific, three-dimensional living spaces, the work was more challenging. Two semesters in, my favorite professor, Rod Underwood, made an offhand comment about my work. "This is great. But when you got to this side, you just took a flat design and pulled it out to make it three dimensions." I knew he'd recognized a truth about my limitations, one I'd already seen myself.

Now what? I'd chosen this program because it was highly respected, but that year Ball State was named one of the nation's top party schools, and it seemed obvious to me that if I changed majors I should go elsewhere. My parents knew I wasn't happy, but they declared that changing colleges was out. I had been awarded a full academic scholarship from the Ball State Honors College, and Mom and Dad didn't want me to walk away from the money or opportunities that provided. All of my friends were in architecture with me. They were fun and creative. There were so many things I loved, but deep down, I knew I didn't fit there.

After class one particularly discouraging day, I was sitting in the concrete stairwell just outside the design studio I shared with the other freshman architecture students, when my professor sat down with me. I quickly wiped away tears, hoping he didn't notice.

"Have you ever thought about graphic design?" Rod asked.

"No, not really," I replied. I didn't add what I was thinking: *He must think I can't do this.*

"Look. You can do anything you want to do. You have the

talent. But if you don't love architecture, you shouldn't do it." My tears started flowing again because he understood. "Give graphic design a chance, Kelly. I think you'll love it."

To tell the truth, I wasn't sure what graphic design was, but I trusted Rod. He sat on the committee that had awarded my scholarship, so he knew my background and that I was a strong student. I'd always thought being a good student in academic subjects like math and English obligated me to study something considered academic, not creative. Rod's comments pushed me to look in a direction I wouldn't have otherwise considered.

I quickly discovered that Rod was right. I was giddy with delight every time a graphic design assignment required me to purchase another handful of colorful markers to draw more type. I was in my element when we learned in class about simplifying the essence of an idea, about using line and form and typography to represent and communicate a message. I discovered the psychology and symbolism of color, how language affected the way a concept was perceived, and the effect of different styles on your perception of an object's value. As I was challenged to weave together the strands of a message, connect seemingly dissimilar ideas, and articulate my discoveries, every part of my brain was engaged, and the process energized my soul.

Not long after changing my major, I realized that graphic design was really commercial art renamed, the same area of study my dad had focused on in the early 1960s. I guess I was following in his footsteps after all.

Now I had the flexibility to add classes that weren't strictly art-related: Italian, French, an honors symposium in geometry, bioethics, even an undergraduate fellowship in mathematics with a professor who studied geometric tessellations on a linear plane (think M. C. Escher's repeating tile patterns). I had art classes—design studios, typography, drawing, painting, ceramics, printmaking, and photography. I even studied in England for a semester. The study-abroad program didn't offer courses specific to my major but exposed me to small-group tutorials, a fascinating culture, and a boyfriend with a British accent. Taking advantage of England's proximity to other places I wanted to visit, I went a month early and backpacked through France, Italy, Greece, and Yugoslavia. I see now what I didn't know then—I was filling my mind with sights and experiences and information, critical ingredients for making creative connections that would one day transform my act of prayer. Of course, prayer hadn't been at the top of my mind then. Or, truthfully, for much of my early life.

My family occasionally went to church, enough that I thought of myself as a Christian—mainly because that was part of the name of the churches we would attend when we went (Ladoga Christian, New Ross Christian). In sixth grade, my friend Peggy, whom I mentioned earlier, was new to the school and invited the ten or twelve girls in our class to a slumber party; it just *happened* to coincide with the night the local Baptist church that Peggy attended was awarding a prize to the young person who brought the most guests to their revival. I wasn't old enough to be cynical yet, so when the pastor invited us to give our lives to God, I answered that call with tears streaming down my face.

Throughout my teens, I made prayer charts on graph paper, writing items in red ink that I would check off every night. I wanted to get an A from God in prayer.

For a few months, Mom drove me to and from Peggy's church on Sunday mornings, but she didn't like it there. She was willing to drop me off, but I got tired of going by myself and stopped before long. Occasionally, I read the Bible Peggy's church gave me to commemorate my baptism, but only the words printed in red made sense to me. I skimmed over the *verilys, thees,* and *thous.* Throughout my teens, I made prayer charts on graph paper, writing items in red ink that I would check off every night: *Now I lay me down to sleep. . . . Forgive me of all my sins, and help me to become more religious. Heal the sick and handicapped. Thank you for everything.* I wanted to get an A from God in prayer, converting it from something abstract into something measurable. (All these years later, when I lie down to sleep or am afraid, this litany still runs through my mind—a never-ending loop—including prayers long since answered.)

In high school and college, when I was afraid, I'd beg that kindly old man in the sky to keep me safe. *Help me pass tomorrow's test. Please don't notice all the things I shouldn't be doing. Please let this boy like me.*

Finally, the right boy did like me. Tim and I met near the end of my fourth year of college (of five). In less than a year, I was wearing an engagement ring. The upcoming wedding bells must have prompted thoughts of church bells, because we suddenly wanted to go to church together.

✳ ✳ ✳

Our plan was to take turns choosing a different church each week until we found something we both liked. I'd always been intrigued by the idea of the Universal Unitarian church, though I'd never been to one. Tim grew up Catholic—parochial elementary school, nuns with rulers, the whole thing—but had spent lots of time partying in his fraternity and working to put himself through school, and in the process, he'd let church go.

The strategy sounded good, but I let Tim pick first and immediately fell hopelessly in love with the ritual of the Catholic Mass.

After completing my BFA in graphic design, I started work as an art director at a large Indianapolis ad agency. I attended RCIA (Rites of Christian Initiation of Adults) classes one night a week at the nearby St. Michael the Archangel Church. Tim learned as much as I did. Sister Pat had an explanation for this. "When you're four years old and you ask why we do this or that, you get an answer suitable for a four-year-old. From that point on, you think you know the answer, so you never ask again. But there's so much more to it than a young child can understand."

I loved learning. I loved exploring.

When Sister Pat asked us to close our eyes, imagining the safest place we could be, I saw myself leaning back, Tim's arms wrapped tightly around me. When she said, "Now imagine that is God," something in me awakened, a desire for a kind of intimacy I'd only just begun to imagine—but still didn't know was possible with God.

After nearly a year of classes, I joined the Roman Catholic Church. On Sunday mornings, Tim and I listened to homilies about Notre Dame's football team as the cold radiated from chiseled stone walls and light filtered across the wooden beams high above us. We'd pray while hundreds were speaking the same words, granting our prayers a special kind of power. I'd kneel, full of respect, certain that our heavenly Father heard us, glad to be part of something important, something big. I'd leave, wishing I could bring that feeling home with me.

Tim and I stood proudly at the baptismal font when Father Wilmoth poured holy water over our beautiful baby girl in the lacy white gown Mah sewed for Katie's christening. We had a family photo taken for the church directory and took our turn carrying the offering plate to the front. But then, when Katie turned two and I was pregnant with Anna, I surprised myself and everyone who knew me by longing for the safety and security of a small town. We moved to Crawfordsville, Indiana, a town of about

15,000 people located twenty minutes from my parents' house. By then, I'd left the ad agency and launched my own graphic design business. Since I worked from home with my baby, I could live anywhere. I chose to be near the kind of babysitters I didn't have to pay (i.e., my parents).

But the modern, mauve church in town didn't have the same majestic feeling as our old church. We missed the jovial priest full of personality and funny stories. We were sad to no longer have an operatic cantor with a deep, booming voice singing the responses. The modern church just never felt right to us, and we were torn. If we were Catholic, we needed to go to a Catholic church. We believed in being involved in our local community.

After much discussion, we changed the question. *Are* we Catholic? Do we have to be? How much did that matter to us? We wanted to serve God (in whatever undefined sense that meant)— no, I take that back. We simply liked the *feeling* of going to church. There was nothing particularly spiritual about it. And we wondered if we could like another church as much as St. Michael's, whatever denomination was on the sign outside.

✳ ✳ ✳

Before long, my friend Tami invited me to her Pentecostal church. I knew that Peggy and her husband, Nathan, attended the church, eventually becoming co-pastors a few years later. Tim and I decided to give it a chance. You couldn't find a place more different from our beloved Catholic church. Grace & Mercy Ministries had bloodred carpet, a shiny white podium, and gold and crystal chandeliers. A tall, dignified man in a royal blue suit was leading worship, the platform was full of musicians and singers, a woman named Sandee played the tambourine, and Lady Miller danced her bejeweled fingers across the piano keys while people raised their hands in the air and danced and shouted things like, "Hallelujah!" and "Glory!"

I was afraid. Very, very afraid.

But here's the thing. It was as though something immediately grabbed hold of me and wouldn't let me go. *Now* I know it was the Holy Ghost (as the Holy Spirit is called in the King James Bible they use at this church). At the time, I wasn't sure what it was. But I remember Nathan preaching one Sunday, pacing the carpeted floor, back and forth, stopping and looking right at me. "Do you know Jesus? I mean, know him personally?"

Umm, well, let me get back to you on that.

I found myself drawn back to the church again and again, not really sure why because I felt uncomfortable and off-kilter the whole time I was there. One week, I particularly liked the song they were singing. Upbeat, loud, full of life, with gusto. I am not what you'd call a good singer. Even my husband, who loves me unconditionally, would rather not listen to me. A thought flitted by, unannounced and uncensored. *God, I wish I could sing like that for You.*

And then I heard it: "I JUST WANT YOU HERE."

I could hardly breathe. I didn't want to move, afraid I'd lose that moment. I'd never heard from God before.

From that point on, I couldn't get enough of God, and within months, I told my friend Lisa that I was pretty sure Tim thought I needed an intervention because I was attending church three times a week. And a crazy charismatic church, no less. He went with me some weeks, though, and before too long, without us really discussing it, we were going together every Sunday. One morning, someone at church asked Tim what he was giving up for Lent that year. Without missing a beat, he responded, "The Catholic church!"

He said that—and I relate the story now—not to be mean.

Truly, we don't have a thing against the Catholic church. We—Tim especially—just have a sarcastic sense of humor. Underneath it, though, a truth came through. We were both happy at Grace & Mercy Ministries. We'd found whatever it was we were looking for, in the most unlikely of places. Not where we thought we'd end up, yet exactly where we belonged.

Because it was all so new and different to me, and because I had grown up believing (forgive me, please) that religious people weren't very smart, I struggled. In college humanities classes, I'd learned that the Bible was literature, full of symbolism and relevant simply as a record of history. At this church, they took it seriously. *Literally.* I didn't know the basic Bible stories, so I bought a children's book to learn them quickly.

Since I didn't have a strong church background, I was in a foreign land. And I wanted someone to bring me deep, thorough, intellectually sound answers—not the ones meant for a young child. I questioned many of the fundamental premises, refusing to accept something to be true just because someone said so. So I debated. And debated. And questioned. And raised my hand in Sunday school. And bought several different Bible translations. And challenged my friends' and pastors' opinions. And started reading books from Christian bookstores, researching different teachings and denominations, trying desperately to understand. I wanted the type of assurance that so many people at my church demonstrated, the kind of faith that was unshakable. But I didn't have a personality that could just blithely accept an answer that wasn't rooted in fact.

If God existed wasn't ever a question for me. I don't know why. I just believed. I'd hypothesize, just for the sake of argument, that maybe He didn't really exist. But the worst-case scenario for me, even if I ultimately discovered that it was all a myth, meant that I'd lived my life with some sort of purpose, following a set of ethical guidelines. It wouldn't hurt a thing, even if I was wrong. Even if it was a delusion. But I never seriously believed it could be one and hoped that God wouldn't be mad at me for wondering.

I *wanted* to believe. But I couldn't do it blindly. I'd spent my whole life learning to examine things. My training in (and exposure to) art rooted in me the desire to look—really look—at everything I saw. My academic background (and my mom's side of the family, populated with doctors and nurses and cynics and people who put education first) wouldn't allow me to simply take faith at face value. Not long after I started attending Grace & Mercy, I wrote in my journal that I felt like a translator; I was here to observe, to see things and figure out how to translate them so they made sense to someone on the outside. Of course, at that time, I was the outsider.

> I'd spent my whole life learning to examine things. My training in (and exposure to) art rooted in me the desire to look—really look—at everything I saw.

For the next few years, I studied. Read. Prayed. Explored prayer. Marveled at the insights I found. Learned to hear God's voice. My third child, Bobby, was born, my husband started teaching children's church, I audited a college class on memoir, and I began to use writing to try to express the truths I'd found in God. In that class, the instructor gave us a writing prompt one day: *Write the letter you would never dare send.*

Mine was directed to my mom, which began, "I don't know how you, who have known me my entire life, can so completely *not* understand me." As much as I loved her, I was tired of the disapproval about my newfound faith I sensed from her on the other end of the phone line when I would call. "You're going to church again? Isn't once on Sunday enough?" My grandfather had been head of radiology at a Catholic hospital, and Mom always liked the nuns and the rituals. Once I joined the Church, she attended Mass with us whenever she could. She liked it. But now this idea of "selling out" to God? Letting faith guide you? Going to church for two hours on Sunday morning, three on Sunday night, having lunch in between with people from church, and being sad if a school activity kept us away on Wednesday night? That was alien. Uncomfortable. Maybe even slightly cultish.

Kerry and Doug were married at the Methodist church across the street from the house we later sold to Rosanne. They got serious about their faith about the same time that Tim and I began to get involved at Grace & Mercy, inviting us to attend a weekly Alpha class with them to learn more about the basics of Christianity. We got to see firsthand how the personality of that church fit them. Then, to our surprise, Mom found her place at the Episcopal church, loving the Altar Guild and intellectual debates with her priest. Dad stayed home on Sundays—he'd grown up in the Church of God, and it was fine that Mom went, but he only accompanied her on holidays.

Suddenly, most of my family—who had only gone to church erratically for the first thirty years of my life—was in church. Churches. Because we all seamlessly fit in such disparate places, I guess I never thought to question that. I didn't understand the way that some people, including some people I knew and respected, could believe that only one style of worship, one way of living for God, was right. I saw my family's lives expand. I saw multiple groups open their doors and embrace us. I soaked up the differences and marveled at how big God was. That He was big enough to span all these places, all the different rituals, structures, practices, and variations of beliefs, and still reign supreme over it all.

I attended Bible studies with Lutherans, Presbyterians, Baptists, and people from Calvary Chapel; prayed with people from contemporary, crowded churches with electric guitars and from small country churches whose chipped hymn boards announced that number 224 was up next. I had deep spiritual discussions with a friend who was raised Jewish, and I recognized glimpses of the God I knew in the God she described. I compared my method of praying with that of my non-Christian friends, atheists and agnostics and universalists, who—with great love and compassion—sent positive energy, prayed to the universe, and held me close in their thoughts. I wasn't offended by different perspectives; instead, I was touched by the love motivating their actions. And I saw my God—Himself the author of love—in all of it.

When I realized that God had me praying upside down, just like Betty Edwards's students were taught to draw upside down, it opened the door to lots of connections. I looked for God everywhere—and found Him in it all. When I opened up books on art, all I could see was faith. It was like a movie sequence, where the detective suddenly puts together all the pieces of the mystery. In the space of thirty seconds, flash cuts of one image on another on another put the story together for the audience. That's how it felt to me—and then I put words to something I'd already felt deep inside—that art mirrored faith. That our God is the original Artist and Creator. That there is a beauty present in God that so many people miss because they don't know to look for it.

Praying upside down is any way that God shakes you out of your comfort zone. It's a new perspective, an attitude of exploration, the wonder and marvel of sacred revelation.

I fell to my knees in awe that He had allowed me to see it.

As I made the connection between different art techniques and types of prayer, it became clear that this art thing wasn't a gimmick. It was truly the way I saw my faith. The way I lived it. There was a beauty and simplicity and profound truth to it that I couldn't deny. I discovered that some of the techniques I'm going to explain are more literally upside down than others—but that praying upside down is any way that God shakes you out of your comfort zone. Any way He opens your eyes. It's whatever helps you see Him and His active presence in the events of your days. It's a new perspective, an attitude of exploration, the wonder and marvel of sacred revelation. This idea is a solid foundation on which to build a lifetime of prayer. And it's available to you, too. I promise.

✳ ✳ ✳

Fast-forward to today, whatever day it is that you are reading this book. As I write this, I'm looking through tear-filled eyes, grateful for each one of you who are reading these words. And my heart expands with hope, with possibility, knowing the wonder of that singular moment when God stretches your mind and allows you to see beyond the physical world in front of you. I'm asking Him right now to let you see. To open your mind in a new way. To blow a purifying wind into the closed-off parts of your heart, whisking away the debris we all carry with us. To let you bring all of your hurts and doubts, cynicism and fears with you. To not be afraid to ask the hard questions. To know that He is big enough to handle it all. Big enough to question, big enough to trust.

And creative enough to show Himself to you in a different way.

As you begin to pray this way, embrace—and *expect*—the unexpected. Prepare to be turned upside down. Your faith will never be the same again.

*My dad has learned to see the beauty in the ordinary,
and his work reflects what he sees.*

CHAPTER 5

SEEING WHAT'S THERE
(REALISM)

I have no special talents. I am only passionately curious.

ALBERT EINSTEIN

If there's one thing I know, it is this: Art intimidates people. Ask the person sitting nearest you in the coffee shop, passing you on the sidewalk, or in the next office at work if she can draw. Nearly every time, you'll hear, "I can't even draw a straight line."

Why would you want to? I mean, how often do you really *need* a straight line? Curvy ones are so much more interesting.

In this book, we'll focus mainly on one type of art, realism, which is exactly what it sounds like—an attempt to accurately portray the subject matter. This genre is about *representing* what you see, rather than *interpreting* it. There are many approaches, and we will study those techniques that focus on truthfully representing what is in front of us and then apply them to prayer. I've discovered that you will change your prayer life when you learn to see God. When I seek the truth, I find more of Jesus, just as He promised: "And you will know the truth, and the truth will set you free" (John 8:32).

When you let go of the idea of having to pray with straight lines, you're asking God to show you a new reality—His. By not limiting your discovery to what you imagine or assume to be true, you will cut through prejudices and assumptions and judgments. Look objectively at your motives. Since you cannot hide the truth from God, it's better to face your doubts and ask the tough questions.

My favorite verse in the Bible is from the Gospel of Mark, when Jesus is asked to heal a boy, and the boy's father cries out, "I do believe, but help me overcome my unbelief!"[2] It has been in those moments when I didn't hold back, when I told God how much I hurt, how desperate I was to understand an apparent contradiction, how much I longed to get closer to Him, or how much I resented His answer—when I faced the truth, no matter what it was—that God's answers changed the way I saw Him. And changed who I am.

* * *

We relate to realism because it is familiar. You may know what a Norman Rockwell, Andrew Wyeth, or Edward Hopper painting looks like. The prints on your doctor's walls or in a hotel room may not always be high quality, but there's a good chance that they're representational—showing something we can recognize and understand. Modern art is a different story altogether; many of us don't get it. The giant painting on the museum wall, according to the tiny plaque next to it, is a groundbreaking, significant work that changed the face of modern art. To us, it may just look like a big red square. Or a grid with a couple of squares colored in. Or maybe paint splatters very similar to those made by your toddler. *Even I could've done that,* we think. And maybe that's true.

But one aspect of modern art is particularly relevant to prayer. Modern art is remarkable, not because of the skill with which the brushstrokes were applied to the canvas or the selection of colors or even because of the accuracy of the drawings, but because the artist portrayed something new.

These works are mostly celebrated because the artist saw his subject in an innovative, unconventional way.

> *Modern art is remarkable because the artist portrayed something new. These works are mostly celebrated because the artist saw his subject in an innovative, unconventional way.*

Did Picasso paint his portraits so that you could pick out his subjects strolling down the street? We'd probably freak out if we saw someone who resembled what he put on canvas. The person in Edvard Munch's *The Scream*—if taken out of the painting and placed in a dark alley—would cause us to scream too. Salvador Dali didn't use actual melting clocks as models for his paintings. The work of these artists is prized not for its accurate representation of the physical world but for the way it shows a feeling or emotion or idea in a new way.

Art doesn't have to be your greatest talent in order for you to make art. It's all about practice, about your willingness to keep trying, over and over again. If you don't observe your subject matter carefully, though, you won't improve. Truth is at the heart of all art and all prayer. Even in abstract, nonrepresentational art, the artist is often using the tools at his disposal to elicit some kind of truth in the viewer—an observation, an insight, an emotion, a feeling, a reality—even if it looks nothing like the object that inspired it.

People who are adept at drawing are actually displaying a heightened sensitivity to visual facts. Drawing is a language, and if you don't know the words, you won't be able to speak. To draw well, you must learn to see facts such as size, shape, and color. By paying close attention, you'll start to notice the details—a splash of vivid colors, the underlying form giving shape to an object (is it a sphere? a cube?)—whether you're looking at the original object right-side up or upside down. The more you practice, the more accurately you will see.

The same goes for prayer. You've got to keep your eyes wide open to see what God is doing. No special talent is required. There is only the act of prayer—which in its most basic form is simply communication with the Almighty—and practice.

The idea of communicating directly with God may be intimidating to you, even more so than the thought of creating. But don't let fear hold you back. God wants to hear from you. Everything Jesus did and said while on this earth points to the fact that He came to build relationships. He turned no one away and welcomed everyone.

Yes, even you. *Especially* you.

* * *

For some reason, airports bring out the worst in me. As I watch each person walk by, I find myself thinking things like, *Must be nice to be able to afford a beach vacation*, or *No wonder she's successful, wearing such a low-cut blouse and those spike heels*. Or *Look at that rock on her finger. She must be loaded.* I'm embarrassed to admit how judgmental I can be in an unguarded moment, even though I can honestly say status symbols mean very little to me. Except, apparently, in an airport. Sadly, it takes a while for me to pull myself back into line, and usually it happens as I realize, *Hey, I'm going someplace, too.* And, *Oh yeah, I just bought this suit at Macy's so I'd look the part for the meeting tomorrow, because they probably wouldn't take me seriously in sweats.* And, *Well, I have a decent-sized diamond, too, not because we're wealthy but because it's a stone (with a giant flaw inside) that has been passed down through four generations of my family.*

Humans are a curious mix. Those of us who are not convinced of our worth never feel we measure up. Those of us with pride issues might believe we deserve more than others. The fact of the matter is that we're all in the same boat—often swinging between the two extremes within minutes. Every single one of us needs help overcoming whatever particular issues we have. But those issues won't keep God from drawing near to us.

Jesus addressed this very thing. To the Pharisees who judged the poor company He associated with, Jesus replied: "Healthy people don't need a doctor—sick people do. . . . For I have come to call not those who think they are righteous, but those who know they are sinners" (Matthew 9:12-13).

And to the Jews, who believed the message was exclusively for them, the apostle Paul stated that it was for everyone. "We have all been baptized into one body by one Spirit, and we all share the same Spirit" (1 Corinthians 12:13).

God welcomes each of us equally, turning no one away. He loves, wants, and accepts us all. No matter what I think when I'm at the airport.

✳ ✳ ✳

Maybe you know God welcomes you, but you're not sure exactly what qualifies as prayer. You wonder if you know how to do it right. Don't let yourself be limited by someone else's definition of prayer. Be open to the possibility that prayer will look different for you than it does for a friend, maybe even like nothing you've seen before. Prayer can happen when you're alone with coffee at 5 a.m. in a blessedly silent house or late at night when the kids are in bed. On the nights when your spouse works second or third shift and there's no one around but you and God. In a circle during Bible study, squeezing hands to pass the prayer to the next person, or gathered with your family around a grave on a hot sunny day, when the heat of the sun can't evaporate the tears as fast as they fall. Listening to worship music in your car, not wanting to stop driving when you reach your destination so you circle the block two or three more times. On your knees during Mass, when you're suddenly aware of how much bigger the Lord is than you and how powerful it is to pray with hundreds of others. In the collective silence of a Friends meeting. Or from the front row of an evangelical church, reveling in the upbeat music and emotion swirling between the upraised arms.

Prayer may take place as you lie facing away from your husband in bed, trying to hide the sounds of your crying as your heart breaks for a friend—or for yourself. Sitting on the porch swing, listening to the birds and feeling the breeze, silently talking to God about your day. Shaving your legs as you ask God to guide your steps that week. Flat on your face in your bedroom in the middle of the morning when you get a call about a tumor in your friend's son's chest. Spontaneously gathering around a friend during book club, when her sadness about infertility becomes your own and as a group you reach out to God together.

Prayer can take place around a campfire with marshmallows melting on sticks and acoustic guitars strumming. Or on a train in the midst of a sea of commuters. In line at the drugstore, while the elderly woman in front of you discusses the complicated side effects of her husband's blood pressure medication. It doesn't have to happen at an early hour, on your knees, Bible open

Expect that prayer will look different from year to year—or day to day. Prayer is fluid, and your relationship with God will change over time and through different situations.

before you. It doesn't have to happen in the church sanctuary, although it can. Prayer is not limited by time or place or even by the one who is praying.

Don't worry if your prayer doesn't look like your best friend's or your sister's or your boyfriend's or your father's. Expect that it will look different from year to year—or day to day. Prayer is fluid, and your relationship with God will change over time and through different situations. It may not always be pretty. It may feel hectic and disjointed; you may start praying in the shower and then get distracted and not finish until you're waiting for the water to boil for spaghetti at dinnertime. The good news is that God always shows up when you look for Him.

* * *

When my kids were little, I read an article that changed the way I parent. The advice for building confidence in your children was simple: Praise your child only for what he has actually done. Don't exaggerate. Say to your son, "The cat you drew looks really happy," not "You're going to be the next Picasso." Tell your daughter, "I love to watch you do cartwheels," not "You're going to be an Olympic gymnast someday." When you set unrealistic goals for your children, you're setting them up for feelings of failure and inadequacy. These same feelings get in the way for us as adults when we contemplate trying something new, whether in art or prayer. And while your child may not make it to the Olympics, maybe she really does a pretty good cartwheel. That's okay. It's enough. You can believe in her and encourage her and teach her to work hard and try new things—and she'll be able to tell that your praise is genuine.

Reading this book does not mean you're the most spiritual person alive or that you will out-pray everyone you know as a result. You don't have to have high expectations for yourself. Instead, be proud of yourself simply because you're here. It says that you are willing to consider something new. That you want to learn more. And that, when you picked up this book, you didn't think, *This upside-down thing is crazy*— or especially if you thought it and are giving it a chance anyway.

Just showing up equals success. It means you want to grow closer to God, start getting to know Him, or, possibly, figure out if He is real.

You don't have to pray like I do. I don't like rules, and I don't want prayer to feel like a chore. I want you to find your own way, and I hope that praying upside down helps you do that. In this case, just showing up equals success. It means you want to grow closer to God, start getting to know Him, or, possibly, figure out if He is real. Whatever your goal, I believe God always rewards our efforts to find Him. Do your best to silence your inner critic, because that voice gets in the way of most artists—and stops many pray-ers before they even get started.

There are countless ways to see God, His influence, and His active presence in your life. God made us all with different personalities and sensibilities, so each of us brings something unique to the table. I hope that as you learn about these approaches, one might ignite a passion for intercession or illuminate a new facet of the heavenly Father or direct you around a roadblock you hadn't noticed before.

Praying upside down may not change your world. But it can change the way you *see* your world by transforming your experiences *within* your world. And it can change *you.*

✳ ✳ ✳

My friend Callie called me one day. "You're not going to believe this!" Although she normally left early for work, she was home one morning because her daughter's school started late that day. As they prepared to leave the house, Callie went to adjust the thermostat. As she did, she looked up and noticed that the crown molding was shimmering with heat. She didn't smell smoke, so she calmly called 911. They told her to grab her daughter and evacuate the house immediately.

It turns out that the bulb in the kitchen pantry had ignited, and the fire leapt upward. The flames spread along the beams spanning the length of the house. Everything below the roof (but above the ceiling) was burning, yet the fire was completely hidden. Except for that shimmer that had caught her eye. The firemen told her that if she'd waited another ten minutes to call or if she hadn't gone back to turn down the heat, the whole house would have combusted.

While Callie was grateful she'd responded to the nudge to call 911 and that her family was safe, the next few weeks were difficult. Her family wasn't allowed back inside the house. Callie, her husband, David, and their three children (all under the age of eight) had to live in an extended-stay hotel. Because their clothes and furniture had sustained smoke damage, everything was being sanitized. Each family member bought a couple of new outfits at Walmart, and there was much time spent at the Laundromat. Mornings were especially hectic as they maneuvered around each other in the tiny kitchenette and bathroom. Callie would then hurry to work, returning to cook dinner, bathe her kids, and try to make their temporary quarters feel like a home.

As I scrambled to get my kids out the door in the mornings, I imagined what was happening with Callie. *This can't be easy.* I called her to see how everyone was doing.

"You know," Callie said, "if someone had asked me if I would be willing to relocate my family for twelve weeks while someone came in and redid my house with all new carpet, new wood floors, and new paint in every room, I would have said, 'Absolutely.' I'd be thrilled. So, that's how I'm choosing to see this: as a blessing."

I can't say for certain that I would have seen it that way, but I love that she did. And by doing so, she turned the situation around for her family. Living in a hotel became not an inconvenience but a step toward something really good. Instead of pitying their circumstances, they were excited about the new things that would come from this "bad" situation.

Like so much in life, the way you see it determines how you live it. The truth is that Callie's house almost burned down and her family lived with great inconvenience for a quarter of a year. But the truth is *also* that Callie's sweet girls are still giggling and alive. That they're all unharmed. That her house was repaired and updated beautifully, and the renovations she'd always longed for—but wasn't able to afford—were completed in three months, without her husband having to pick up a hammer.

Every coin has the potential to offer you heads or tails. When looking to see which it is, keep your mind open. Don't jump to the same old conclusions. Consider unusual perceptions—and look closely. You won't be the first to discover that something new and surprising is hiding right in front of you.

✳ ✳ ✳

Horses have long been a subject of artists, going back to early cave paintings. Because of the speed with which horses run, though, artists had difficulty judging the positions of their legs. The logistics of a horse's stride were a subject of debate for decades. Usually, horses were depicted with front legs stretched forward and hind legs extended to the rear. In 1872, former California governor Leland Stanford hired photographer Eadweard Muybridge to take a series of still photographs of a horse in motion to settle this debate once and for all. Muybridge's images proved that while all the legs were off the ground simultaneously, this occurred only at the point in the horse's stride when his legs were underneath him. At no point during a gallop are the horse's legs extended ahead of and behind the horse at the same time.

Horses running were an everyday sight, but no one had observed reality well enough to settle the discussion. It wasn't until new photographic techniques captured the actual movement that this inaccuracy was deciphered. The truth surprised nearly everyone, because reality didn't match their assumptions.

If the idea of facing the unexpected frightens you, if that takes you way beyond the edges of your comfort zone, well, take a deep breath and know you're not alone. Ray Bradbury said that living with risk is to "jump off the cliff and learn how to make wings on the way down."[3] In other words, this is a good place to be, right on the edge of a new discovery.

Even so, it can be a bit intimidating to start something new. This is especially true if you're creating art. That blank canvas . . . so much possibility.

Possibility or pressure?

It depends on why you're creating it, I suppose. If someone hired you to create a masterpiece, if you have a large commission that depends on your success, or if people are actively watching you—*that* can be intimidating. If you have to complete something specific and you have exactly one canvas, or a limited amount of paints or time, that might cause some trepidation.

Luckily for you and for me, this book is one place where the pressure is off. You are not here to perform or to achieve—just to *do*. Art is interesting because of the individual styles, the variety of techniques, and the differences in approaches. Whatever you create in prayer, one thing is certain: You *will* get God's attention. He's waiting, as eagerly as you are, to see what will happen when you work together.

> *Art is interesting because of the individual styles, the variety of techniques, and the differences in approaches. Whatever you create in prayer, one thing is certain: You* will *get God's attention.*

Realism is relevant to prayer because we live real lives. And we serve a real God. Focusing on the truth of what we see, feel, and experience is one way to find the very real presence of God in every moment. This contradicts what some of the world believes, and naysayers may use words like *coincidence* and *luck* to interpret the same events. But that makes the truth no less true. It only means we need to open our eyes a little wider, craning our necks if necessary to see around the assumptions that block our view of reality.

Because with God, the possibilities are endless.

PRAYER PALETTE

I believe in Christianity as I believe that the sun has risen: not only because I see it, but because by it I see everything else. ~C. S. LEWIS

BE AN OBSERVER. Being an artist starts with observing the world. Slowly look around you. Take your time. Let your eyes linger over each individual thing. Does an object you see bring up a memory or idea? A name? A thought? The idea is not to make a list of the things in your line of sight, but to use these external images as connections to the subject of your prayers as well as to God Himself. As you look, pray for the person, situation, or concern that comes to mind. Your prayer can be as brief and heartfelt as simply saying thank you. You can also use this time to reflect on what happened in your day and to look for God's presence in each interaction and situation. Ask God to illuminate your thoughts and help you see Him.

SHIFT YOUR PERSPECTIVE. My friend Sharon has a "flip side theory," which is the idea that there's always another way to reframe things, particularly in relationships. For instance, when you think about what frustrates you the most about your spouse, you will often find that it's another side of the quality that first attracted you to him or her. Sharon gives the example of her dad, whom she describes as being so righteous and never wrong, but the flip side is that he is incredibly strong-willed and believes his convictions. He couldn't be one without the other. It is helpful to consider the flip side of a person or situation and see if that changes the way you deal with it.

TURN IT AROUND. See if you can find another way to look at the reality before you turn your prayer upside down. Look at the other

57

people who might be affected by the same conditions or who might benefit from the things you are hoping for. Start your prayer with this: "Lord, allow me to be part of something bigger, something that will help other people too." And then look for ways to turn it around. Here are some ideas.

I'M STRUGGLING FINANCIALLY.

- Show me how I can give more generously.
- Pray for the person who will be blessed by finding just the right house/car/job.
- Expand my competitor's business or territory.

I'M STRUGGLING AT WORK.

- Give my boss (or coworkers) new opportunities.
- Put me where I can make the biggest difference to someone else.
- Help me improve the atmosphere at work for the people I work with.
- Bless the users of the product we make/sell and allow the company to expand.

I'M FLOUNDERING SPIRITUALLY.

- Renew those around me; fill them with contagious passion.
- Move the leaders and mentors in my life into the roles you've planned for them.

I'M SICK.

- Help me make this a positive experience for my caregivers.
- Show me ways to encourage someone else in a similar situation.

I'M UNHAPPY IN MY RELATIONSHIP(S).

- Make it clear how I can better provide for their needs.

- Help me to bless my spouse with kindness, forgiveness, better communication skills.

I'M LONELY.

- Prepare me to be the friend, business partner, or family member someone else is praying to have come into his or her life.
- Show me who else in my life is lonely and how I can help them.

What do you see first—profiles of faces or a goblet?

CHAPTER 6

WHAT'S BLOCKING YOUR VIEW?

(OBSTACLES TO SEEING CLEARLY)

Creativity is the power to connect the seemingly unconnected.

WILLIAM PLOMER

When you stare at the chapter-opening image, what do you see? Two faces in profile, or a goblet? In 1915, a Danish psychologist named Edgar Rubin developed this optical illusion. At the time, this was groundbreaking because it exemplified the fact that our brains can only focus on one image at a time—we see either the black goblet or the two profiles. In order to see one, you have to stop looking at the other. Yet there's no denying that the illustration contains both elements.

In this example, as in daily life, it's up to us to interpret what our brains tell us. Is your child crying about having to eat a single green bean, or is it really about how tired he is from staying up too late last night? Are you furious with your husband for leaving the refrigerator door wide open, or is your frustration stemming from the ridiculous deadline your best client just gave you?

If we look closely, we may see more than what first met the eye. Often, though, we see only what we expect—when drawing, when questioning, when praying. Our preconceived ideas get in the way, hindering accuracy, clarity, and spiritual growth—limiting how much of the truth we are able to see.

I've heard numerous people in the church—and friends outside the church—talk about the fact that when they were in the worst trials of their lives, God had never felt closer. They were hyperaware of His presence as they dealt with a scary diagnosis, or watched a brother die too young, or signed the papers that turned their wedding rings into meaningless pieces of jewelry. My friend Suzanne often says, "I want to be as desperate for Him as when I was desperate." In other words, even though the outward circumstances were terrible, a 7 or 8 on the stressor scale, the intensity with which she felt God inwardly was wonderful. She wishes she could feel that close to Him without being in the midst of such despair.

Me, too.

There was a time when I noticed that God seemed to be preparing me for rotten situations by first allowing me to experience lovely, deeply personal times with Him. I was on cloud nine—touched by His sweetness—until some wacky part of my brain decided that even though the times with Him were good and made me strong enough to endure what would follow, maybe if I'd skip the good times I could also skip the bad.

After all, why would I put myself through these times willingly? It was easier to just avoid spending time with Him.

That was one of the most illogical conclusions I've ever drawn.

* * *

When my mom was diagnosed with metastatic small-cell lung cancer in 2008, we started a roller-coaster ride—a few ups, with several months of remission to celebrate but many more disappointments that kept us plummeting downward on what seemed like the world's longest ride.

At the same time, it was way, way too short.

At least I'll get to experience God with a new intensity, I thought. *There has to be something redeeming in all of this.* I remember lying on the floor in front of the altar in my empty church that first week, tears dripping onto the Bible I'd placed under my head as a pillow. I looked up at the shadowy platform, the empty chairs and microphone stands, wordlessly desperate for God's sustaining comfort, His electrifying presence, His overwhelming love. *Zip.* He'd always spoken when I sought Him. He was *always* there for me. *So why did I feel nothing when I was begging for my mom's life?*

I prayed less and less often on my own, but I asked for prayer during every church service, prayer group, and Bible study when there was a new hurdle my mom was facing. I said the right things, declaring that God was able to heal my mom. He was. He is.

But the dirty little secret I dared not speak aloud was that I was convinced He wouldn't.

The truth I already sensed is that while God always answers our prayers, we don't always get the answers we want. He *can* heal, but He doesn't always. In my mind, I understood that lack of healing didn't mean God wasn't there.

My heart, though, shouted otherwise.

Is it my fault? I wouldn't even let myself wonder if God would have done more if I believed more. If I prayed more.

I tried to accept what my mom said herself, right after she was diagnosed: "I'm sixty-seven years old. This may be sad, but it's not tragic." Tragic is watching my neighbor Mike place his six-year-old son's body in the back of the hearse parked in our driveway, fighting to remain standing as the funeral director quietly closes the door between him and Henry. It is a mother giving birth to her third child and dying a month later from malignant cells consuming the body her kids and husband still needed. Tragic is tsunamis wiping out entire villages. Gang wars and drive-by shootings. Kids who take guns to school to try to quiet the demons in their minds. Tragic is *not* a retired woman with a fatal disease.

I knew what my mom meant, but still my agonized soul screamed that this was the most tragic thing I'd ever experienced. It didn't matter that I was in my forties and had my own kids. We were talking about *my mom*.

As Mom went through chemo and radiation and continued to receive news we didn't like, I tried to deny the feeling that God had forsaken me. During the last few months of her life, our family's emotions would level off just long enough for us to try to catch our breath before we'd hurtle downward again, leaving our stomachs behind. The fact that we knew the inevitable outcome—and had three years to prepare for it—didn't make it any easier to come to terms with it, because when it finally came, I had lost my mommy.

Intellectually, I knew God loved me. Intellectually, I knew He answered prayer. I'd seen enough real-life examples of things that could not otherwise be explained. I had to believe. Nonintellectually, I harbored quiet resentment, and before long, I found myself rolling my eyes when people talked about how *their* prayers had been answered.

Goody for you, I thought, sulking like a teenager who hadn't gotten her way.

I tried, over and over, to connect with God, but I couldn't see past the walls I erected between myself and the One who didn't give me what I wanted. And surely it wasn't my responsibility—I was the victim here, after all. *He's God. Shouldn't He be able to get past a teensy little wall I built?* The abandonment I struggled with seemed to be an appropriate punishment for my lack of faith.

> *I tried, over and over, to connect with God, but I couldn't see past the walls I erected between myself and the One who didn't give me what I wanted.*

God never changes. But, boy, our perceptions sure do. Why do we make things so complicated?

I'd always felt like I had a special relationship with God. When I looked for Him, I found Him. I remained open and vulnerable—childlike, I suppose—when I went to Him, and He responded with intimacy. I never questioned the access He freely offered me—until He didn't heal my mom. I started to wonder, *If He doesn't do good things, is He still good?* I didn't think I could talk to Him about that. Nor was I sure I wanted to. I couldn't make myself care enough about anything else to pray, and I knew if I opened up to pray about losing Mom, I would fall apart. I had zero interest in being vulnerable. My heart ached at the mere suggestion. With each decision and inability to pray, I wrapped myself in another layer, encased alone in a brittle, protective shell.

"Don't close yourself off. Lean on God," Peggy advised me. I nodded as though I would do just that. "Honey, I don't think you realize how close to the end your mom is," my friends Sherry and Lisa said, gently, over lunch. "Yes, I do. I really do," I said, lying through my teeth and crying during the drive home. In my defense, I didn't know I wasn't telling the truth.

When I prayed, *if* I prayed, I was just going through the motions. No two-way conversations for me, just talking and no listening—because (1) I knew I was being stubborn, (2) I didn't sincerely believe God would answer, and (3) I didn't like what He might have to say to me about my attitude.

I was falling apart. God knew better than anyone how much I needed Him. And still He'd left me all alone. Why didn't He overwhelm me with His presence in my darkest moments? My sister, Kerry, who was facing the same outcome as I was, remained strong. She got up early and read her Bible. She still trusted in the power of prayer. But I couldn't find Him or see Him in any of it. Whenever I heard someone say, "God is good," I thought, *Yeah, right.*

Not my most shining moment.

Leaks

Six months after we lost Mom, I would still crumble in the least likely places—like in the cleaning products aisle at the grocery store, when a teacher who worked with Mom told me she missed her. Or when a friend would complain, just as I always had, about her mom driving her crazy. Or several times a week, when I thought, *That's what I need! To call Mom!* I kept Kleenex boxes in every room (and in my car) and never left the house without waterproof mascara. I still got up on Sunday mornings and stood in my usual spot at church. But I couldn't make myself attend my favorite service on Sunday evenings; the thought of smiling and making small talk made me weary. So weary.

One stormy Sunday morning, I could hear water pouring in through a hole in the fellowship hall next to the sanctuary—still leaking, after months of attempts to fix it. *They really need to do something about that.* Then, *If they had the money, I'm sure they would fix it.* Moments later, *Maybe I should give them some—a couple hundred? Nah. We give plenty.*

I missed most of the rest of the service, busy arguing with myself. We had finally paid off nearly all of our debt from our home renovations and were doing okay. We had a little extra. Donating money wasn't a direction from God, just a nice thought. I like extravagant gestures, and I wanted to see the faces of our good friends and pastors, Nathan and Peggy, when I told them this thrilling news. I decided to check with Tim first, when he finished teaching his Sunday school class, but I was sure he'd agree.

That morning, a visiting preacher spoke about living on the fresh word of God. He likened it to manna, which God provided to the Israelites in the desert exactly once a day.[4] Every morning the ground would be covered with manna, and the Israelites could eat their fill. It provided the exact nutrition they needed. But the people were warned: Don't store it up. Anything not used on the same day would become infested with maggots and decay.

"God speaks continuously. You just have to listen," the preacher declared. Maybe we had heard from God fifteen years earlier when we started coming to church, or maybe God helped steer us in a certain direction a week or a month or a year earlier. "That's fine," he said. "But it shouldn't stop there. God intended for our faith to be living and active. We need to seek a fresh word from God *every day*." He paced behind the podium, then stopped and turned to face us. "What have you heard from Him lately? What will He speak to you *right now*?"

I leaned my forehead onto my folded hands. *God, I've lost touch with You. What do You have for me today? Speak to me.*

And then I heard:

"SUSTAIN THE HOUSE OF GOD AND I WILL SUSTAIN YOU."

My fresh word. Both a sacrifice and a promise.

The voice wasn't audible; it was a wordless thought, exactly how it had happened when God told me to pray for the woman who would be buying my house. In that instant, I understood layer upon layer of meaning which superseded the literal meaning of the words, and hinted at purpose and insights that were much bigger than the words themselves.

This is what I knew: I would give the church $1,000 for the roof—it had to be a large enough amount to be a sacrifice. (My idea of extravagance doesn't measure up to His.) But even more important, I needed to go to the church every day for at least a month. I would sit in the empty sanctuary, with a new journal, praying through every Bible verse about the house of God—fifty separate mentions. Not only could I intercede for our church and its people, but this would help me reconnect with God, because writing has always been the fastest and most direct way for me to hear from Him.

Even in those first moments, I knew this wasn't about the physical structure of the building, but what the building represented: the home of our faith. A storehouse. A place of provision. A meeting house. A place of renewal. A symbol of our collective spiritual life. A place of communion and fellowship, sacrifice and servanthood, kindness and generosity. A source of help. A lighthouse to the community. A symbol of my renewed commitment to the Lord.

I felt such relief. Finally I could stop focusing on Mom.

My Daily Sustenance

The next morning, I looked up the word *sustain* in my concordance[5]: "To support or maintain; to keep in existence." And then I read the Scriptures containing that word.

"I laid me down and slept; I awaked; for the Lord sustained me" (Psalm 3:5, KJV).

"Cast thy burden upon the Lord, and he shall sustain thee" (Psalm 55:22, KJV).

I was on the floor at the front of our church, copying these verses. I'd been in that same spot three and a half years earlier, the day Mom called with the devastating news. God had been so silent that day. But now there was a sense of peace enveloping the room, weighty and majestic. More tears fell onto my Bible, ones of relief, not despair.

He was here with me.

It suddenly became clear. *When You asked me to sustain Your house, God, You weren't talking about repairing a leaking roof at all.* He wanted me to see that my relationship with Him had eroded and was caving in—and that He wanted to fix it. I didn't have trouble going to Him on behalf of someone else, but I was skittish and unsure about the welcome I might receive approaching Him with my own requests. I'd forgotten that the umbrella of God's whole church also encompassed me. First Corinthians 3:16-17 says: "Don't you realize that all of you together are the temple of God and that the Spirit of God lives in you? . . . For God's temple is holy, and you are that temple."

As the apostle Paul says, in God's upside-down way, He took religion out of a building and placed a temple inside His people. The God of the Unexpected always hears the cries of our hearts before we say (or don't say) the words. And He deals with those issues first, before answering a specific request. What I needed—not what I *wanted*, but what I *needed* to sustain my faith—was a fresh taste of God. A new perspective. Because I couldn't see clearly from where I'd been standing.

In the garden of Gethsemane, as Jesus prepares to endure an unthinkable agony, He prays, "My Father! If it is possible, let this cup of suffering be taken away from me. Yet I want your will to be done, not mine" (Matthew 26:39). I've always believed that "this cup" refers to the roles God designed each of us to fulfill. What He has for us, what we have to endure. As I lay on the floor, I saw the whole truth of the Rubin optical illusion: When we come face-to-face with God, a cup is formed between us. Jesus Himself didn't like what God placed in His cup—yet He trusted God's ways.

This was my cup. But it could only be borne by standing face-to-face with God.

Through bleary eyes, I wrote:

*You know how lost I am—how without-a-home I feel.
Since Mom died, I've felt untethered, no anchor, nothing
to center me. So You had to remind me that You are
the Sustainer. You've given me—or, really, reminded
me that I already had—a home. And that You've been
there all along. You've reminded me that Mom does
not define me, You do. I thought I'd be praying for this
physical structure, these walls, this building—that we
would work from the outside in. But You work from the
inside out.*

Inside out and upside down.

That explained the problem with my prayers—God's answers didn't match the ones I wanted, so I concluded that He wasn't who I thought He was. *Losing Mom couldn't be the right answer, so You must be wrong.* But I was applying His answers to the wrong questions. It was as if I were looking at a blue wall and refusing to admit it was blue because I wanted it to be green. I had decided my world would never feel right again without my mom and that wasn't okay with me. Turning toward God was like saying it was.

I thought that if I prayed, I was a hypocrite. If I claimed God was good when I thought He'd done badly, then I was lying. Or deluded. I can see it as clear as day now: God standing right behind me, arms stretched wide open, never leaving my side, crying along with me, absorbing my pain as His own. Waiting patiently for me to turn and see Him, to realize He'd been there all along. He would

> *God was standing right behind me, arms stretched wide open, never leaving my side, crying along with me, absorbing my pain as His own. He'd been there all along.*

never make me turn. I needed to do it myself. That's how His grace works.

I didn't see Him there because my eyes were closed tight.

Actually, God *did* answer my prayers. As a family, we had tightened our circle. Living next door had made it easy for Kerry and me to help with each other's kids when the other drove Mom to chemo or radiation. Mom and Dad could stop by whenever they were in town and see us both. Mom's love for us—and ours for her—was a given. The petty aggravations that had always had me slamming down the phone and shouting *"AAARRGH!"* no longer burdened me. One blessing of cancer: You let go of the little stuff that doesn't matter.

We thought we would only get a year or so, but we had three more years with her. My parents held hands wherever they walked together. Mom made Dad buy a sports car because she wanted him to have something fun, and it would prevent gossip about his misuse of insurance money if he bought one later. Dad had the chance to be her rock, remaining unwavering and steady as she became more and more wobbly.

Mom cursed her scratchy wig. She despised being and looking sick. But she served as a court-appointed special advocate anyway—always helping kids—and cheered her grandkids in soccer, swimming, baseball, theater, tennis, and basketball. The decline was very slow until the end, and then it came rapidly, with a huge answer to prayer. For three years, she'd been afraid of the end. She was a nurse, and she knew all that could happen to her body. She was petrified by the thought of suffocating as her lungs ceased to function. Instead, her whole body quietly gave out as she took slow, deep, peaceful breaths. She died at home, in the place she loved.

Love. Family. An awareness of what we had. And, finally, freedom from pain. How had I ever convinced myself God wasn't present?

✳   ✳   ✳

In the illustration at the beginning of this chapter, the goblet and faces share the same edges. You'll see one thing or the other, depending on how you look at it, but the secondary object always remains because it can't exist without its counterpart. When you sit down to pray, you're only hurting yourself if you impose limits on God or set arbitrary guidelines for how God should behave. I learned the hard way. I was looking at the goblet (the events that were poured out) and denying the flip side—God's face. In your situation, God may answer the way you expect Him to. Or not. But even when the answer isn't what you hoped, you might be surprised how closely connected His answer is to your prayer. It's just a matter of looking at the same thing—often what's sitting right in front of you—from an unexpected point of view. Sometimes that means having to stretch your neck to see past a big, ugly hurdle.

But what you'll see at the end makes the stretch totally worth it.

PRAYER PALETTE

I will have nothing to do with a God who cares only occasionally. I need a God who is with us always, everywhere, in the deepest depths as well as the highest heights. It is when things go wrong, when good things do not happen, when our prayers seem to have been lost, that God is most present. We do not need the sheltering wings when things go smoothly. We are closest to God in the darkness, stumbling along blindly. ~MADELEINE L'ENGLE, GLIMPSES OF GRACE

When you're having a hard time praying, try something different. Prayer doesn't have to fit the stereotype of head bowed, knees bent, eyes closed. In fact, it doesn't even have to consist of words.

DOODLING. When words don't come, let your pen or marker wander. Write down a name. Pray for that person, or simply offer up the silence and act of moving your pen as your prayer. Draw around it. Make shapes, fill in sections with color. Outline, underline, cross out, write in other names. Each line you draw is a prayer. When you move to the next shape or word, surrender the first one to God and trust that He hears your heart. Your doodles are a tangible record of your prayer focus, just as if you wrote out every word in sentences.

CARTOONING. A cartoon is a simple drawing showing exaggerated features. Drawing a scenario as a cartoon helps you clarify the dominant features or characteristics. When you show them larger, smaller, greater, better, or worse than they really are, it helps you note what's important. Draw yourself. Draw your situation. How can you represent the stumbling block that is in your way? Where you draw God—or how, or if—can tell you a lot about how you feel.

You can do a similar thing with words. Write a fairy tale about real-life circumstances, complete with heroines and villains and extreme consequences. It will help you see more clearly the main issues and won't feel like prayer. Just remember, it's a safe bet that you're not the real hero in this story. But that doesn't prevent you from being the faithful sidekick.

A child's point of view may be quite different from an adult's.

CHAPTER 7

WHERE ARE YOU STANDING?

(POINT OF VIEW)

The question is not what you look at, but what you see.

HENRY DAVID THOREAU

A little boy looked up at David Slonim, a children's book illustrator speaking to his class, and asked a burning question: "How come you never draw nostrils?"

From where David stood, he saw the cute little turned-up top of a child's nose. The child, however, peered straight up David's nostrils. The question provided David with a new perspective—whose point of view is the story from, anyway? This newfound empathy enabled him to connect more closely with the children who were his audience and lent a new authenticity to his illustrations.

Where we stand in prayer matters too—profoundly. Sometimes we approach God with unfounded assumptions that limit what we see. It's important to see what's in front of you, true. But it's also important for you to notice where you are standing at any given moment because your viewpoint affects what you see. Are you praying from a valley or a mountaintop? Looking up or down? What brought you here? What experiences, prejudices, or hurts led you to this particular vantage point?

> *No man ever steps in the same river twice, for it's not*
> *the same river and he's not the same man.*
>
> HERACLITUS

I've always thought of my church, particularly the sanctuary, as a safe place. The safest of the safe. I am free to worship how I want, whether it's standing with arms extended, kneeling before the altar, or sitting with eyes closed in the pew. The people—and the building itself—seem to wrap me in a protective embrace. As I enter into each service, I feel the tension in my shoulders ease, my breaths deepen.

One morning, as I stood in my usual spot, letting the words of the praise song wash over me, a man walked in and sat in the pew in front of me. When I opened my eyes, I froze. What was *he* doing here? Even if he recognized me, which I doubted, he probably wouldn't remember the night I met him twenty-five years earlier. I knew I'd never forget it, though. In an instant, my mind transported me right back to that moment.

When I was in high school, I hung out with the wrong crowd. People who partied hard. Boys who expected too much. I was a good student—and, other than plenty of now-regretted fights with my mom, a pretty good kid. I didn't break (many) rules. But I made quite a few stupid choices, and I had a weakness for bad boys. One night, I had gone on a date with a guy I barely knew. My criteria weren't all that tough to meet: He had long dark hair; tight, faded jeans; a black Led Zeppelin concert shirt. And he'd asked me out. Good enough.

He drove me to a house at an unfamiliar edge of town. I was the only girl there, and he and his friends smoked some pot and drank some beer. I didn't do drugs, but nearly every guy I dated did. At one point, the guys at this party decided to go out for more alcohol. I don't really know how it happened, but there wasn't room in the car for me. They drove away, leaving me alone with Rich (not his real name)—this man who was now sitting in front of me at church.

That night he prowled around me, spewing vile, demeaning names. He raised his arm as though to strike me and ordered me to get him another beer. He delivered a graphic play-by-play of the horrible things he was going to make me do. To this day, I can't figure out how or why I ended up in that house alone with a stranger who chose to abuse me this way—or why he didn't follow through with his threats. All I remember is cowering in the corner between the wall and the refrigerator, shaking. The other guys came back and laughed at my tear-streaked face while they opened more beers, and eventually my "date" took me home. I rushed past my parents so that they wouldn't know anything was wrong and kept this ugly memory all to myself.

In all the years since, even though I'd never seen Rich again, the knowledge of what *could* have happened terrorized me. And the shame that I hadn't done anything to get myself out of that situation. Once the immediate threat was removed, I felt really, really stupid. If that had been the only questionable night of my rebellious years, maybe it wouldn't haunt me the same way. But memories of that time in my life bring back, if not shame, then at least regret. Sorrow for the girl who didn't think she deserved better. Who didn't know how to give herself better situations, better friends, better chances.

In the past twenty-five years, I'd discovered God. Now I sit in the second row each week, dressed up, an elder of my church, hands raised in worship. My husband sings with the praise and worship team. My kids run free, carrying around other people's babies, as comfortable here as at home. A rebel now only in my mind, my teen years were miles behind me. Miles. And yet, my heart pounded and knees trembled to see Rich trespassing in my safe place. *Mine.* He did not belong here.

God had already forgiven me for my past. When we confess our sins, His forgiveness eradicates them, once and for all.[6] I hadn't done anything wrong that long-ago night. The sight of Rich, though, made my stomach hurt and my hands shake. I closed my eyes to make him disappear, but then the revulsion and shame suffocated me. In desperation, I prayed. *Lord, forgive me for the choices I made. Forgive me for my rebellion. Forgive me for the anger and hate I feel. I'm so sorry for the person I was. I try to pretend I've changed, that I'm a better person, but I'm not, am I? I'm a hypocrite. I can't hide. You know who I am—how bad I am—at the core.*

That day, instead of the still, small voice that sometimes

whispers to me in peaceful times, God spoke over my mental anguish, loudly enough to quiet my soul immediately.

"YOU ARE NOT THE SAME PERSON ANYMORE."

This truth overwhelmed me. It didn't matter what that teenage, misguided girl did (or didn't do), because God no longer saw her when He looked at me. "Anyone who belongs to Christ has become a new person. The old life is gone; a new life has begun!" (2 Corinthians 5:17).

I am certain I will make many more foolish, potentially dangerous choices in my lifetime. But the shame? It didn't belong. Shame is to faith what oil is to water. They don't mix. I'd chosen long ago to set aside fear, replacing it with faith. My dirty little secrets did not define me. They lost their power over me once I handed them to God.

But I did have to open my eyes, eventually, once the music stopped. I hoped the service would never end, but I couldn't escape soon enough. I tried praying for Rich, thanking God for the changes He'd made in this man's life. It hadn't escaped my notice that we were *both* in church that day, a scenario I wouldn't have imagined twenty-five years before. And I knew that God was just as willing to forgive this man as He was to forgive me (and He quite possibly already had). I prayed in an effort to rise above it all—while mentally planning my dash to the doors the second the last piano notes were played. I grabbed my Bible bag but was stopped by another church member who was reaching for my hand. "Kelly, I want you to meet somebody. This is my friend Rich. He's in from out of town."

I shook his hand, dared to make eye contact, smiled—and managed not to throw up. No spark of recognition. *Whew.* I walked away.

I was so caught up in my own little world that I hadn't realized there were other perspectives to this story as well.

I later learned that not long after that traumatic night in high school, Rich got married. Although he and his wife were not together long, their marriage marked the beginning of a rocky, hard life for her. Physical abuse, addictions, rehab, destructive relationships, a broken heart. Again and again. In recent years, I've gotten to know her. She's generous with her encouragement and praise. Deeply reliant on God. Open about her failings. She dances at the front of her church as only someone who fully understands the extent of her need for God could do. God saved her life. She is victorious through Him who helped her get past the fear and shame and sorrow.

Knowing her reminds me that, while I'll never forget the fear I felt that night with Rich, it was only one night—nothing compared to the fear that permeated her life every single day. God gave me a new perspective, just like the kid who saw nostrils from where he was standing. The beauty of that child's observation is the fact that he noticed. He kept his eyes open. So I pray for my friend, asking the Lord to continue to heal all the broken places. I grieve for all that she lost and all the scars that she still carries. I'm thankful for the extravagant love she shows, the same love that God lavished on her—and wants to share with me.

✳ ✳ ✳

"But I say, love your enemies! Pray for those who persecute you!" (Matthew 5:44)

Talk about upside down. The fifth chapter of Matthew is filled with unlikely proclamations—blessed are the meek? The poor in spirit? Those who mourn? And then the chapter ends with the idea of loving your enemies and praying for those who persecute you?

In Luke's Gospel, Jesus went a little further, addressing those who wanted an eye for an eye, always countering hate with hate:

"But to you who are willing to listen, I say, love your enemies! Do good to those who hate you. Bless those who curse you. Pray for those who hurt you" (Luke 6:27-28).

It's not easy to pray for our enemies. I won't pretend otherwise. First off, we don't want to like them. After all, he or she slept with your spouse, or drank too much whiskey before ramming his or her car into your cousin's, or lied about you to your

> *It's not easy to pray for our enemies. I won't pretend otherwise. First off, we don't want to like them. What kind of God would expect you to pray for those people?*

boss, or stole from you, or raped you, or cheated you, or turned your son against you, or sabotaged a business deal, or bullied you, or_____(fill in the blank).

What kind of God would expect you to pray for those people?

Ours. The One who is so full of compassion, so genuinely good and loving that He knows that if He lets you keep that resentment inside of you, it will tear you apart from the inside out.

Many years ago, my friend Kaiya's[7] husband was unfaithful to her. He surrendered to God, and they were able to rebuild the marriage—with God at the center this time—into something even better than before. From the start, she decided to forgive her husband and the women he was with. But several years after that, a mentor of hers figured out who one of the women was and said, "You say you've forgiven her, Kaiya, but I think you need to pray about whether you need to ask her forgiveness. I've seen the looks you've given her, and I don't think she feels very forgiven."

Kaiya prayed but wasn't compelled to take action. But God kept pushing her until, after a couple of failed attempts, she caught the woman, Laura, at work. Kaiya said she needed to ask for her forgiveness, because although she'd said she forgave, she kept taking it back. As they hugged and cried together, Kaiya felt the burden of the unforgiveness she had carried fall away.

About a year later, Kaiya saw Laura at a restaurant. Laura pulled Kaiya aside and said, "I really want to thank you for forgiving me and asking my forgiveness. I didn't realize how much of a block that had been." Laura had battled some devastating health blows shortly after the two of them had met, but she admitted to Kaiya, "Getting right with you helped me get right with God."

God wasn't done with Kaiya yet. There was a second woman, Kim, with whom she needed to make things right. She hadn't crossed paths with Kim for years and then, suddenly, she saw her three times in one week. "This one felt dicier," Kaiya told me. "Kim didn't know me."

Kim ran a local small business, so she wasn't hard to find once Kaiya decided to go to her. Kaiya walked into Kim's office and said, "Years ago, I proclaimed that I forgave you, but since I've seen you three times this week, I've realized there's ugliness in my heart. And I'm pretty sure that you didn't see the loving eyes of God or feel forgiveness when you saw me. I'm here to ask forgiveness for my attitude."

Kaiya's words seemed to release something in Kim. She told Kaiya that she was wrong and she was sorry, and they cried for an hour as Kim talked about how confused and self-destructive she'd been in her life. Kaiya explained that we're all sinners, and when we accept Christ, He wipes all that away. That's the beauty of God. All of us are undeserving and need forgiveness. No matter what happened in the past, God is the One who will always be faithful. Kaiya grasped Kim's hands and prayed, and later mailed her a Bible. She never heard from or saw Kim again.

When Kaiya told me this story, she said, "I don't know if she's a believer. I don't know. But that's not my part in this." Her part was to obey the little pushes she felt from God, to act in a way that is upside down from the norm. "God took the mustard seed's worth of repentance and sorrow in me and was gracious enough to work with me. That helped her and it helped me."

Sometimes, even if we're the one the world sees as the victim, God asks something that seems to tilt our world even further off its axis. But these women? They had been hurt, too. Until Kaiya came to them, they felt stuck, torn apart by the knowledge of what they'd done. It took her faith that God would not lead her astray, and her up-close knowledge of the situation and the pain involved, to give her the courage to do the unexpected. To show them a gracious God. He is ultimately the One who has the power to forgive, and He does, without hesitation, if we will ask. But sometimes we need to hear the words in an audible voice. Sometimes we need a face and emotions and the warmth of a person in the same room in order to understand that the forgiveness is real. To accept what we so badly want but are afraid we can't have.

As Kaiya demonstrated, if we want it, we must first offer it. "If you forgive those who sin against you, your heavenly Father will forgive you. But if you refuse to forgive others, your Father will not forgive your sins" (Matthew 6:14-15).

We don't have to like what happened, and we don't have to become best friends with the people who have hurt us. But when you bow your body, and in turn your spirit, in the presence of the Most Holy, you realize that God sees the whole thing differently. You realize that even if you don't think a person deserves forgiveness—well, truly, neither do you or I. The word *deserve* doesn't enter into the equation of grace.

James 5:16 tells us, "Confess your sins to each other and pray for each other so that you may be healed." That is what I want. Healing. The change that comes when I pray for others.

A part of me wants to be self-righteous, to believe that I don't have to pray for Rich because that was the past. I've moved on, and so should my prayers. But I have learned that God often turns things around, and He doesn't make random, meaningless requests. His ways aid healing, bring forgiveness, and soothe the hurting places. He gives us power to help ourselves.

And sometimes that comes in the form of allowing us to see reality. Deep in the hidden recesses of my heart, the God of grace says no words. He simply shines his purifying spotlight on the feelings I've stuffed back in a corner of my heart. I see how ugly they are. I see that I haven't forgiven. That I'm not loving the way God does. That I am flawed, and wrong, and that this isn't about Rich. It's about me.

God often turns things around, and He doesn't make random, meaningless requests. His ways aid healing, bring forgiveness, and soothe the hurting places.

So I sit down again, fall to the floor in sorrow and worship and praise, and I pray for him. I pray with new insight for my friend who was hurt by the man who threatened me, and I pray for me. And I hold tight to the belief that, in this imperfect attempt, perfect healing will come.

* * *

My friend Suzanne often talks about the fiery darts that Satan shoots at us.[8] We can't stop the darts (of accusation, shame, temptation) from coming our way. But we do have a choice—to grab hold of these condemning thoughts and gnaw on them awhile, or to move aside and let them sail on past. Unpleasant memories will jump out at us from time to time. Temptation will come our way. We don't have to feel guilt when the thoughts flash past—but it's up to us not to catch them and carry them with us. We can certainly use the darts to our advantage, though, because knowing where we have been, where we are now, what we've carried, how far we've traveled, and what we've learned gives us the ability to pray with fervor and insight for another person.

Ask God to use your pain for a greater good. And in the process, when you face your grief, fear, pain, or sorrow from a new angle, when you put yourself in someone else's position, don't forget to pay attention. Look around. Try to see what they see, nostrils and all. It could change everything for everyone.

PRAYER PALETTE

Not being changed by prayer is sort of like standing in the middle of a spring rain without getting wet. It's hard to stand in the center of God's acceptance and love without getting it all over you.
~STEVE BROWN, APPROACHING GOD

MAKING CONNECTIONS. STEP 1: Write down some of the biggest challenges you've faced in your life. Include the big events, the ones that have changed you, helped you grow, held you back, or moved you into a different life stage. Label them in general terms—loss of a parent/spouse/child/friend/home, medical conditions, extreme financial situations, end of a marriage, job changes, difficult life decisions (education, career, finances, relationships), addictions (drugs, alcohol, pornography, abusive relationships), a child leaving home, legal issues, losing or gaining weight, infertility, infidelity, bullying, moving (or buying or selling a home).

STEP 2: Ask God to guide you as you look over your list to see what you've been through that will help you feel compassion for someone else. Write down the names of people who come to mind. List them beside situations you have in common—are you both divorced? Have you both nursed an aging parent? Have you struggled with the same challenge as your friend? Don't try to stay on track. Let your mind follow those rabbit trails, and trust that God is leading you where He wants you to go. Draw from your own emotions, memories, and experiences to put yourself in the place of the person for whom you are praying.

PRAYER JOURNAL FOR A SPECIFIC PERSON. One year, I wanted to offer Peggy something different for Christmas. I knew she believed in the power of prayer, but I wanted to put my prayers in a form that was more tangible. So I bought a thin, pretty notebook, and every day for a month I wrote out my prayer, focusing on a different aspect of her life each day: her children, husband, family, ministry, finances, health, and spiritual journey. Peggy was blown away—because this gift showed her the time and effort I'd invested in it. She saw how much I valued her friendship. I was blown away by the way that praying with such purpose for a specific person opened up my heart to connect with her in a new way.

WRITTEN PRAYER FOR A FRIEND. This is a smaller-scale approach to the prayer journal idea. When someone e-mails me a prayer request, or when I just have a person on my mind, I will write out my prayer as I pray it and then send it to that person. This shows that you took the prayer request seriously and followed through on your promise to pray. Your e-mail, text, or written note becomes a meaningful representation of your prayer. Use your own personal experiences to give you insight into how to pray for each person.

Even though the snow isn't painted, negative space allows us to see it.

CHAPTER 8

LEAVING ROOM FOR GOD IN THE PICTURE

(WHITE SPACE AND NEGATIVE SPACE)

Prayer is not monologue, but dialogue; its most essential part is God's voice in response to mine. Listening to God's voice is the secret of the assurance that He will listen to mine.

ANDREW MURRAY

I've always loved my dad's hands. Large, strong, capable, and gentle. Soft but not frail. So much talent hidden there. My dad went to art school, but before that he worked with his father, a cabinetmaker. He became a skilled carpenter, creating things both solid and aesthetically pleasing. But when he sits down with an artist's brush, I find myself amazed every time. He has such a delicate touch—in a few strokes, he can effortlessly invoke the sagging roofline of a barn in the snow, bring out depth and dimension in the shadows of a hollyhock, or carve ruts in a dirt lane. With years of experience and loads of innate talent, Dad makes it look easy. When people ask him how long it took to paint a painting, he answers, "Three hours and thirty years." (He's said that for so long that it really should be "three hours and fifty years," but that's not as catchy.) He invested the kind of time that only someone who loves what he is doing can give. As a result, his skills have become second nature, a process that barely requires thought. It's not that easy for the rest of us.

I think my dad's landscapes are beautiful, but his talent is perhaps most evident where he does *not* apply paint. Most people focus on the objects themselves, the positive space, but Dad has learned how to define a scene using negative space (the area around and between objects). His signature paintings consist of weathered, rickety barns resting in the snow. Due to their composition (the way they are placed on the page), the objects are balanced by the white of the paper so that the viewer focuses on the barn, roof, and wobbly fence undulating across the barnyard. This negative space is powerful because our brains fill in the blanks—we recognize the white area, the part left untouched, as pristine snow. The absence allows us to focus on the presence.

Amateur artists will often fill in every part of the canvas, carefully and painstakingly rendering every little thing. Taken by itself, each object may be exquisite. But when you look at the whole, your eye doesn't know where to rest. Because there's so much to see, nothing stands out.

In art—as in prayer—sometimes less is more.

White Space

The majority of people (including me), interchange the terms "white space" and "negative space," although they're actually different things. Negative space is the area or shape formed by surrounding objects. White space is the part of a page that is left unmarked. In Dad's paintings, both terms apply. The unmarked areas define the marked.

In graphic design, white space refers to the margins, the space between paragraphs and photographs. Even though it contains no objects, the white space has an important role in the overall design. Clients try desperately to fill this space, not realizing that the more they squeeze in, the less any of it stands out. And the less room there is for the viewer to draw conclusions.

At a community prayer meeting I once attended, a facilitator distributed handouts telling us how to pray. The needs were very specific: "Clear the blood of sepsis; no bronchiectasis; get her off the ventilator in no more than two weeks," and ended with a request for a "Clear diagnosis of cilia immotility or CF and then complete healing of either diagnosis."

I know there's not a right or wrong way to ask God to intervene. Their hearts were in the right place; they were praying full of faith that God would answer, and to be honest, I don't remember how these prayers were answered. But that night, the mode of prayer taught me more than the answer. As I closed my eyes, all I could think was, *Lord, I am not smart enough to tell You what to do or to address every possible complication. I don't really care how You heal her. I just hope You will. Let her know You are with her. Heal her body and heal her soul.*

Jesus said this world's self-professed prayer warriors are "full of formulas and programs and advice, peddling techniques for getting what you want from God. Don't fall for that nonsense. This is your Father you are dealing with, and he knows better than you what you need. With a God like this loving you, you can pray very simply" (Matthew 6:7-8, *The Message*).

It felt to me that the supplied prayer list was a case of leaving no white space, no room for God to respond. We were coating the canvas with thick, gloppy paint, leaving nothing to the imagination. I couldn't shake the feeling that we were setting ourselves up for disappointment—if God didn't answer our prayers just as we had stated, would we still think He had answered? It also hinted at the possibility that maybe we didn't think God was omniscient after all, because wouldn't He have already known the problems and all the potential ramifications? And, ultimately, the best way to take care of it?

> *There is nothing wrong with praying in detail. But there's no value in using a bunch of words just for the sake of making sound. The bigger picture is found in silence. In listening.*

There is nothing wrong with asking, with praying in detail. The Bible tells us, "Don't worry about anything; instead, pray about everything. Tell God what you need, and thank him for all he has done" (Philippians 4:6). But when we don't have all the right words or know how to solve the problem, that's okay, too. The Bible assures us that the Holy Spirit helps us pray by interceding for us.[9] But there's no value in using a bunch of words just for the sake of making sound. The bigger picture is found in silence. In listening. God implores us to "Be still, and know that I am God!" (Psalm 46:10).

Our culture has virtually drowned out quiet time. TVs and radios play nonstop, and visually—as well as audibly—they take up space, with more spectacular graphics and faster transitions to appease our society's ever-shorter attention spans. T-shirts advertise bands and causes while bumper stickers, window decals, and vinyl graphics shout to us from cars and trucks. When many of us do find a moment of peace, we pop in a pair of earbuds and let our favorite tunes fill our heads until the latest text chimes or a phone call transports us back into our noisy world. We are a culture of instant gratification and excess. Every surface, every moment, is filled to capacity. We grow uncomfortable when a silence stretches too long.

Maybe it's time we let it. Who knows what we might hear in the white spaces?

Filling in the Gaps

Sometimes the gaps are already there, providing an opportunity for God to fill them. But other times we need to carve out space and invite Him into it. I'm not saying that if you empty out your bank account, God will fill it. He might, but if that were a common occurrence I think we'd hear more about it (and see a whole lot more generous giving).

My church operates a food pantry. Our weekly church attendance is around 150, but we feed hundreds of families a month. A dedicated group of people works diligently to stock the pantry with quality nutritious items and then opens our doors to the community three times a week. One day the church was notified that, because of our track record, we were going to start receiving government surplus foods at no cost. We were ecstatic.

Free is always good.

My pastor, Nathan, heard about an industrial-sized upright freezer for sale. Suspecting that we would be feeding more people as a result of having more food available, and knowing that we already needed more storage for the frozen meat we purchased for the food pantry, he attached a trailer to his truck and drove forty-five minutes north to get the freezer. When he returned to the church's parking lot, he felt God speak to him: "Why did you just get one?" There were actually two of them for sale.

Nathan didn't question whether he was hearing from God. He just said, "I wish you'd said something sooner," unloaded the first freezer, and headed back for the second. Nathan handcrafts beautiful leather goods on the side, and it just so happened that he had sold a surplus industrial sewing machine the day before and had a pocket full of cash (enough to pay for both freezers).

That evening, the church received a call from the local Walmart with an unexpected offer. In an effort to cut costs and distribute their excess food with the greatest efficiency, they were no longer going to transport their near-expiration-date groceries to the regional food bank located forty-five minutes away (the place where our church had been purchasing the items for our food pantry). Instead, they wondered if we'd like to get it directly, eliminating the middleman.

Also for free. Three times a week.

The next day, our two new freezers—and all other food pantry storage spaces—were filled to the brim. Frozen meats by the vanload. Tables heaped with breads, cakes, cookies, and rolls. Crates of produce just past its peak, but still perfectly good. We are usually overloaded with lots of good food that we are able to pass on to those in need of immediate help. God's church has become a storehouse in action.

Ask Nathan, and he will tell you it's not luck or coincidence that everything happened as it did. It's simply a case of God filling up a space our church created with the expectation that He would fill it. This is another way that you and I can use white space—create a void and trust/expect/believe that God will fill it in just the right way.

If you're anything like me, your days are packed to the limit and you're laughing out loud at the thought of being able to carve out some free time. Years ago, my friend Karin told me how she combated this—with a black Sharpie. (Gotta love anyone who fights battles using art supplies.) Every morning she looked at her family's calendar, marker in hand, and made choices on the spot about what could be eliminated. She didn't waffle. If, for any reason, it didn't fit, caused other conflicts, or created scheduling chaos, she crossed it out.

Book club at the same time as the swim meet? Don't run back and forth; pick one. Maybe this time you'll choose book club because there's a home swim meet on Thursday and this one is an hour away, or because your friend in book club just had a miscarriage and you want to be there with her. Perhaps in two weeks you'll choose the swim meet because your daughter has been working hard to trim a couple of seconds off her time and you want to be in the stands, cheering, when she does.

Karin looked at planning meetings, committees, volunteer work, kids' activities, and school projects. She weighed them against each other and chose tactically and smartly—but still she chose. She drew a big black line through anything that didn't fit.

I don't do this nearly as well as Karin does. It *all* seems important to me. I have seen God work in my client relationships, in the lives of the people I spend time with, in church activities and Bible studies. It's *all* good. *All* godly. So how do I give something up?

When I questioned Karin about this, she said, "Of course you see God in all of it. He's in *everything*. But just because God's there, doesn't mean *you* have to be there. He can use you in other places, too. Give someone else a chance to be used here."

She's right, but I have to remind myself daily to make choices rather than juggle it all.

My friend Lisa knows a woman whose trusty watch broke. She didn't have money for another one and wondered, *How am I going to get places on time without this?* And she felt an immediate response: *Let* Me *direct your time.*

Novel idea. Ask God how to fill your days, instead of packing them so full that He has no room to move. Keep some white space.

Over the next few weeks, Lisa's friend found that she was able to fulfill her responsibilities even without a watch to guide her. She actually managed to get more done than usual and kept finding herself in surprising situations where God showed up. Try it for yourself. As you finish your shower tomorrow morning, say, "God, my time is yours. Help me trust You to fill it. Help me believe that with You in control, the important things *will* get done." Then dry off. And watch what happens.

> *Ask God how to fill your days, instead of packing them so full that He has no room to move. Keep some white space.*

At the post office, you may see a friend who just had a fight with her husband and needs someone to talk to. At the grocery checkout line, the man in front of you may be three dollars short—and, surprise, that's exactly how much cash you found in the bottom of your purse that morning. When you run into the sports store to get soccer socks for your son's game tonight, you'll find out they're half off, today only. Your smile is the first one the guy behind the counter has seen all day. In the parking lot outside, you step aside to allow the woman parked next to you to get out of her car, and you see that it's a woman from your mom's Bunco club. When she looks at you with tears in her eyes and hugs you, no words, just because she misses her, too, you feel as if you got to hug your mom instead. Because you're not rushing to fill the day with your own agenda, you leave an extra couple of bucks for the server at lunch because you can tell she's having a bad day. One more second, and a small amount of money, is all it took to make a big difference.

Then, when you get back to work, you see that someone who was copied on that e-mail string about tomorrow's presentation was able to find the missing pieces without you having to take time to gather them. As you send up a prayer for a friend whose sister's health is failing, you get an annoying e-mail about a new project that's due by the end of the day, and you're not happy about it, but it's just an ad. Not life or death. The people and situations you encountered today put the exasperating details into perspective.

Full schedules can still feel empty, but the hours you offer God will likely transform them from a bunch of items on your to-do list into days of meaningful, satisfying interaction. You will feel God because you found time for God. Because you offer Him your time, He will use it. His time becomes that of the cashier behind the counter at the sports store and your mom's friend and the man who was three dollars short in the checkout line. Layer upon layer of fullness.

The negative space, in other words, allows you to zoom in on the positive space. And because this simpler composition focuses on the things that matter most, you see a different overall picture, better than ever before. Full of blooming colors and vibrant details. You feel the breeze on your face.

And you suddenly find you can breathe again, here in this quiet, holy space. Because you realize it's not empty after all.

PRAYER PALETTE

The principle of art is to pause, not bypass. ~*Jerzy Kosinski*

FINDING TIME. Make a list of "down time" you experience—during a commute, waiting to pick up a child, lunch breaks, sitting down with a cup of coffee in the morning, waiting in lines, sitting in a theater waiting for the movie to start, during commercials when you watch TV, breaks between classes or meetings. Think of these as opportunities to pray. Treat the list like a personal challenge—where can I find more time?—and use it to pray any way you wish.

DRAWING THE LINE. Buy a Sharpie and sit down with your calendar. (If yours is on the computer, print out a few days.) What can you eliminate because it interferes with the way you want to live your life? Gets in the way of what's important? Pushes aside the people with whom you want to have a relationship? Don't jump too far ahead—start with one day at a time. But begin with prayer—*God, where do You want me to be today?* And start marking.

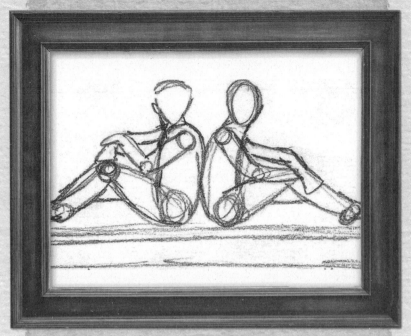

Every complex shape—even people—is made up of a combination of geometric shapes.

CHAPTER 9

WHAT HE IS MADE OF
(DRAWING THE UNDERLYING STRUCTURE)

The very act of drawing an object, however badly, swiftly takes the drawer from a woolly sense of what the object looks like to a precise awareness of its component parts and particularities.

ALAIN DE BOTTON

For centuries, artists have studied the underlying structure of people and objects to improve the accuracy of their drawings. The figures Michelangelo carved look real—as though men are actually stepping out of huge blocks of stone. His knowledge of human anatomy—coupled with, of course, his artistic genius—is what made this possible. It wasn't enough for someone like Michelangelo or da Vinci to draw, paint, or sculpt what they saw. They went to great lengths to understand the body's structure. To study how it worked. Why the hand bends where it does. How the arms and legs and head relate in proportion to each other. They, and many other artists of their time, actually dissected cadavers in order to learn about human anatomy and recorded their findings with detailed drawings. Because they came to understand the *why*, their work was richer and more believable. And in the process of creating their masterpieces, their contributions reached past the boundaries of art into science and medicine.

These great artists knew that they could only accurately render something by understanding what lay beneath the surface. In a more rudimentary way, many artists will examine an object to see its fundamental makeup. Nearly every shape can be represented by some combination of spheres, cubes, cylinders, and cones. If an artist knows how to render those shapes, he can rough in the shape of a complex object fairly easily and go from there to smooth, blend, and refine. They're important building blocks of the final drawing, but those initial shapes won't be obvious and distinct in the final piece. Without them, though, the artist wouldn't have arrived at the same result.

When we pray, we can adopt these pivotal concepts. I use them all the time, whether writing in my prayer journals (more on those later) or talking to God while I wait in the school pickup line. My initial sketch, if you will, begins with the basic shapes. In prayer, I start by outlining the situation in general terms. Not because God doesn't already know, but because it helps get *me* into the right frame of reference. Sometimes, no matter how lofty we try to be, all we can see is the tangible thing right in front of us.

When I tell God about a decision I have to make about work, my fears about a friend's biopsy results, or my hopes for my kids, it reminds me of two things: who I am in relation to God, and how much I need His help. How

> *When I tell God about a decision I have to make, it reminds me of two things: who I am in relation to God, and how much I need His help.*

helpless I am to fix the impossible scenarios in my life. What I'm afraid of, what confuses me, all that concerns me.

And then, possibly as a way to counterbalance my own failings (or, at the very least, my inability to control the universe), I recount His abilities. I switch from talking about me to talking about God (and *to* God). I acknowledge who He is. (*God, You are omnipotent. Omniscient. You are in all things. You are the Creator. You are the Redeemer. You embody mercy and love and grace. Nothing is too hard for You.*) I remember what He has done. (*When Nathan's x-rays showed an aneurysm that was mysteriously gone in the next set, You showed us that You still heal today. . . . When a house contractor refunded us $3,000 unexpectedly, You showed that You provide for us right on time.*)

Before long, I feel the tension seeping out of my shoulders. Fear slinks away as hope comes flooding in. I feel promise. Possibility. My petition turns into praise. Worry gives way to worship.

Talk to anyone who's ever been betrayed (and, really, who hasn't?), and you'll notice the word *trust* comes up a lot. *I can't trust him because he lied to me. I can't trust her because I've seen the way she talks about her friends. I can't trust my employer to reward me for my service, because my managers value characteristics I refuse to exhibit.*

It's hard to trust someone who hasn't proven his loyalty and faithfulness. But God has already proven Himself. If the concept of dying on the cross and raising Himself three days later is hard to wrap your head around, remember that He proves His fundamental nature over and over throughout the Bible. Think of His character as His underlying structure. When we read these stories, we learn about the surprising ways God answers prayers, and we learn about God's expansive love. We witness the sustaining power of a relationship with Him. David is friends with God and seeks Him throughout his life. Whether David is scheming to murder the husband of the woman he lusts after[10] or hurtling rocks at a giant,[11] God welcomes him back with open arms every time. Not because David is great, but because David understands the inherent goodness of God, and no matter what he does, no matter how bad it is, he longs to be back in the presence of the Almighty. He failed royally, yet he humbly worshiped the true King with all of his might.[12]

The hundreds of stories in the Bible are there to portray the character of God. The classic stories illustrated in every children's Bible storybook are just the beginning (and a good place to start if you feel overwhelmed). The Bible reminds us that, for centuries, people have struggled with the same things we do. We've witnessed firsthand these plights in our own lives, and each one of us has his or her own story of coming through them, of being led through them. Pages and pages, volumes and extended collectors' sets, of stories delineating how God is working in our lives.

We can never know for certain whether God intervened in a particular situation or whether it was something like luck. But I've experienced too many times when God's presence has been tangible, when God's fingerprints seemed to be everywhere, to accept that these moments are coincidence. I truly believe it is by God's grace that I wasn't raped that night I was left alone with Rich. When I was newly pregnant with my second child, my two-year-old and I were not injured when a deer ran straight into my Honda Accord on the interstate. I have been handed career opportunities and jobs I wasn't technically qualified for. While I was on a business trip with a near stranger, a writer our mutual client had paired me with, she needed to be rushed to the ER. As I sat beside Sharon in the examining room, our conversations quickly went deep—from health issues such as the breast cancer she had survived to our most private, intense spiritual experiences, ones she doesn't usually share even with her close friends. The conversation continued the next day in between meetings, and now Sharon is one of my dearest friends. When my neighbor showed up at my door begging me to stay with her five-year-old son, Henry, whose grandma had just been rushed to the hospital, I felt compelled to talk to him about Jesus going to prepare a place for us,[13] and what that place might be like. A year or so later, his body wracked by cancer, Henry went to that place himself, and I believe God orchestrated that conversation.

I see God in these stories. And our lives are filled with them. Even in the bad, we have seen good. A friend's hug, a sympathetic shoulder, or a loan of gas money to hold us over until payday. Maybe we've witnessed the depths of love in a marriage even as one half of that couple lets go of life. When I put you on the spot and say "Quick, think—what are your stories?" you may draw a blank. That doesn't mean they're not there—give yourself time to remember. And notice that what we call good and bad are often intertwined. They're not as separate as we'd like them to be. One story can't exist without the other. Like the goblet/faces illustration in chapter 6, life's fullness consists of both.

* * *

One morning, I watched a little girl make the rounds during the worship service. Five-year-old Vanessa is irresistible with her pale translucent skin, dark blond hair, green eyes, and a sweet smile that camouflages her somewhat devious personality. She walked up the aisle with little flouncy twists of her skirt, chin tucked down into her doll, big eyes taking in everything. She stopped at the end of a row, watching until Peggy glanced in her direction. When Vanessa ran to her, Peggy laughed and picked her up and swung her around.

After a few minutes, Vanessa headed to the other end of the row, waiting until Katie beckoned her over. She giggled, snuggling in, prepared to be adored. Just as she was about to doze off in Katie's arms, Vanessa suddenly extended her arms to me. I wrapped my arms around her and squeezed her tight. Before long, she climbed over the pew to sit next to Jordan. When he smiled at her, she scooted closer and showed him her doll, waiting for him to light up in delight. He did. We all had, the moment she shifted her attention to us.

Vanessa was in a safe place, where she knew without a doubt she was loved and would be welcomed with open arms. So she made her way through the church, letting one and all adore her. Because we've loved her since she was born, she knows what to expect. When she leaps into the air, she expects to be caught. When she reaches up, we'll reach down. When she climbs into our laps, she will feel loved. Doubt doesn't enter into the equation. Vanessa feels safe because we've never disappointed her.

God has our best interests at heart. There are no limits to the ways He will solve our problems or the lengths He will go for one, just one, lost or hurting soul.

When we learn the underlying structure of God, we, too, can feel that security. When we read stories about the convoluted paths of men and women failing over and over again—killing and lying and cheating and complaining and rebelling—when we hear about miraculous deliverances, of complete change, of God's unfailing love, then we learn what to expect. We start to believe we can trust Him. We don't know exactly how He'll react—in Vanessa's case, she may not know if we will hug her or spin her or cuddle her or tickle her or give her our last piece of gum—but we do know that He has our best interests at heart. That He's going to do what's right. And that there are no limits to the ways He will solve our problems or the lengths He will go for one, just one, lost or hurting soul.

So we study His Word. We pray. We write. And when the time is right, when we are sure we have His attention, well, then we run toward Him. And leap.

✻   ✻   ✻

Not only does underlying structure tell you about God, it also helps you to know what to pray for. My sister's forty-year-old best friend has stage-four breast cancer—the cancer is spreading, the pain is bad, and the doctors' answers are vague and unsettling. So yes, I am praying, *God, please heal Teresa.* But when I bring in my own experiences, compassion changes things and I start to pray for her to feel God right beside her. To lean back in His arms. To see Him. To not be afraid. For the pain to lessen. When I think about the impact of losing my own mom, I begin to pray for Teresa's children, that they will never doubt the strength of her love for them, no matter what happens, and that other people will step in and fill the family's needs along the way. When I think about the way my dad loved my mom through her sickness, I pray for Teresa's husband to find strength.

It doesn't mean I'm giving up on God's healing—I'm still believing—just that, from knowing God's structure and remembering the events that lie beneath the surface of my own faith, I see more complexity, more nuance. The fact of the matter is, God is in it all, through it all, behind it and in front of it. He is the form on which this world is built. His nature creates a solid base. He never changes.[14] Because we know who He is, because His structure undergirds each landscape, I can let go and let Him have free rein in my life. He instructed us to "pray about everything,"[15] and He knows what we need before we even ask.[16]

He knows. And because, as we get to know Him, we store up memories and examples of what we've seen Him do, we know too. We begin to recognize the basic structure of God, His complexity and strength and beauty. His longevity and goodness. And because we discern enough of what lies below the surface—because we know that we are building on the rock and not on shifting sand[17]—we can begin to paint a more accurate picture.

We will begin to see the shape of God.

PRAYER PALETTE

In art, the hand can never execute anything higher than the heart can imagine. ~RALPH WALDO EMERSON

"I GOT A YELLOW!" My friend Sherry was going through some really tough times a few years ago. Her health was very poor—she was in the middle of a multiple-year course of treatment, and many days she couldn't get out of bed. She lived several hours from most of her family, and she and her son felt very alone. They started filling notebooks with their very specific, finite prayer requests. For example, that she would feel well enough to be able to drink a milk shake that day. Or that they would have the spare money to buy a milk shake. Every day, she and Nick wrote down what they needed, and they prayed. Periodically, they read through the pages with a yellow highlighter, marking every prayer that had been answered. The book filled with yellow.

When, a couple of years later, she moved to our area and attended prayer group, we did the same thing. Every week, we recorded our needs, and then we highlighted the ones that had been fulfilled. Our shorthand for this became "I got a yellow!" This is a great way to build your belief that God really does hear and answer your prayers.

PRAYER RING. Buy a package of index cards and use a hole punch to make a hole in one corner of each card. Every time you hear a prayer request, jot it on a card and attach it to a binder ring. Be sure to write the date on it. In your daily prayer time, flip through them one by one. When you come across one that has been answered, write that date, too, and any relevant details. And watch your faith grow.

WRITE YOUR OWN PSALM. The psalms are comforting to read. They're filled with joy and anger, hope and hopelessness, comfort and confusion, doubt and faith, desperate cries for help and spontaneous overflowing of praise. Ask God to speak to you; then read from the book of Psalms. Find one that touches a chord in your heart, and read it until you understand the writer's emotions—anxiety, celebration, loneliness, praise. Using it as a model, write the same basic lines but personalize it with the specifics of your own situation. Don't worry about form. Just write from your heart, and then as you read through it again, offer it to God as your prayer. Or start from scratch and write your own.

My favorite thing about the psalms is that they don't end in despair. The authors often recount the many ways God has helped them in the past, remembering the underlying structure of God. No matter how desperate the situation, before it's over, the psalmist has found a way to praise, trust, or celebrate. It's a great model for how we should approach God and a compelling form for prayer.

Railroad tracks illustrate where we should always look—toward the horizon.

CHAPTER 10

ALL POINTS CONVERGE AT THE HORIZON

(PERSPECTIVE)

When we focus our minds and fix our attention on Christ, He is magnified and made bigger in our lives. When we focus our minds and fix our attention on life's obstacles, they will be wrongly magnified and made to appear larger than they really are.

LYSA TERKEURST, *WHAT HAPPENS WHEN WOMEN SAY YES TO GOD DEVOTIONAL*

When grief is trying to claw its way out of your heart, shredding your soul as it fights for dominance, when something unspeakably tragic happens, when it's big and shocking and awful and overwhelming, words fail. Thank God we don't need words to pray, that He hears us anyway. Because there are times when my words are broken, stilted, choked. Strangled with pain.

Almost a year ago, my daughter Anna's friend Mike died in a car accident on his way to the high school. A bright, shining boy. His twin brother was driving the truck. Neither had worn a seat belt, and now one is dead and one is alive. Our little community was in shock.

Youth pastors and counselors showed up at schools. Parents opened their doors to groups of grieving kids. Mike was the kind of person who fit in many different places, so many different groups were affected. Show choir. The football team. An organization for teens focused on preventing drug use among their peers. Honors classes. Students from his current high school and the one he'd transferred from a couple of years earlier. So many people. Friends delivered food to these gatherings of kids who were banding together in an effort to make sense of it. But they wouldn't. They couldn't. All they could do was help each other share this load that was too heavy, that wasn't right, that wasn't fair.

As a parent, I wanted to shelter my teenage daughter, shield her from having to feel this pain, having to embark down this road of questioning and aching and sorrowing. Her heart is too tender. This shouldn't happen. But it did.

And for what?

During the same week, another friend of Anna's was in and out of court hearings and meetings with child protective services. When the dad hurt the younger sister this time, the brother called the cops. This sweet girl is bubbly and always smiling, running from friend to friend with encouraging words and hugs. But under it all, she was bearing the weight of responsibility for her siblings, physical abuse, hateful threats, and fear that someone would find out. I had no clue before this. I burst into tears of relief at the news that they got to go to foster care. *Got to.* I was fairly close to the situation, though not close enough to be right in the center of it. But even from where I was standing, it tore me apart, from the inside out.

And then, on the very day all of that happened, my dad had the first procedure to burn off precancerous cells in his esophagus. Two years after losing Mom, this news made me crumple, fear flying in the air between the tests and waiting and words tossed around by doctors. They caught it early, and although the label was *dysplasia*—a precursor to, but not the actual dreaded *cancer*—the procedure was painful, and the recovery longer and more limiting than we expected.

On days like these, when the meanings are lost and emotions are jumbled and hope is battered and it is all too much, all I can do is stand. The words may not come. How do I find hope? How do I go on? How do I pray? What could I even ask for that could matter? I don't know whether to lash out at God or curl up under His sheltering wing. I don't know whether to scream at Him or cry with Him. I just don't know. Because nobody can know. Nobody can do this; nobody can bear it.

Nobody on their own, at least.

There's only One with the strength to carry it. Only One with the depth to understand it. Only One who can see that this is not the end. And that One is not you. Not me.

All we can do is keep things in perspective. By that, I don't mean to find someone worse off than you so you don't feel so bad, although that sometimes helps too. Rather, I'm talking about perspective as defined in art—an artistic technique used to portray depth, to project the illusion of a three-dimensional world onto a two-dimensional surface. If you stand on a railroad track and look as far as you can see, you'll notice the tracks on either side of you appear to get closer together as they move away from you. The light posts that line your street are all the same height, but when you look toward the end of the block, the posts seem to get smaller the farther away they are from you. What you're witnessing is perspective. In order to look natural, the straight edges of any object in a drawing must follow lines that eventually converge at infinity.

When we live a life based on faith, no matter how things appear on the surface, there is always hope. There is always more.

Normally, this point of convergence is along the horizon.

When we live a life based on faith, no matter how things appear on the surface, there is *always* hope. There is *always* more. There is *always* something good. Sometimes we can't see it—when we face a freshly dug grave, hear specialists wielding words like *tumor* or *malignant*, or see bruises hidden beneath a teen's shirtsleeve, we can't begin to wrap our heads around it. All we can do is aim our broken selves in that general direction, pointing toward the Source of that hope. Offering up our pain, trusting that He can absorb it, and that when the pain returns to us, it—and we—will be forever changed. The enormity of the love He has for us will soothe our shredded souls as it floods back in. Filling us. Healing us. Restoring us.

When your heart is broken, turn your face to the horizon. Our perspective is temporal and limited, but God's is infinite and eternal. He sees from on high. One thing that artistic perspective and eternal perspective have in common is this: All points converge at the horizon. And that is where we have to look, because that is where we will find God.

Define Your Viewpoint

Perspective can be defined as "a position in relation to different positions,"[18] or how the world looks from where you are standing. The word *perspective* comes from two Latin words—*per* meaning "through" and *specere*, "to look." In art, what's key to the idea of perspective is the *viewpoint*, the position of the viewer (not that of the artist).

When you are at a low point in the landscape and look up, all you will see is the sky. But when you are standing at a high spot, the different sizes of trees, gentle rolling of the hills, and angles of the buildings contribute to a greater perception of depth.

From where God is standing, He can see a whole lot farther down the road than I can. My perspective limits me, but just over the horizon, hidden from view by the very slight rounding of the earth, may be my answer. My help. I just can't see it yet. Maybe I never will. But if I can get even an inkling of the big picture—either through my knowledge of the character of God or because I've seen a glimpse through prayer—or recognize that He is present because I left white space in our conversation to hear from Him, it becomes easier to believe the answer is out there somewhere.

My mom told me that when I was little, as I watched out the window for company to arrive, I would say, "I *almost* see them coming!" I think this is what is called faith. "Faith is the confidence that what we hope for will actually happen; it gives us assurance about things we cannot see" (Hebrews 11:1). As adults, that sense of expectation, of believing that what we're waiting for is just around the corner, gets pushed aside by worry that there was a car accident or someone ran out of gas or decided not to come. The Bible reminds us that there is a finite season—a time—for each trial,[19] so it follows that there is always an end. When I'm sitting at the window, waiting and watching, I don't have to wonder if my miracle has been lost or if it's been derailed. I can believe that it is on its way. So I'll keep looking down those railroad tracks, knowing that if I do not give up, the answer I'm waiting for *will* arrive. Right on time.

How Close Are You?

We have to pray with our eyes on God, not on the difficulties.

OSWALD CHAMBERS

A fundamental principle of perspective is the idea that, as an object gets farther away, its size decreases. The intervening atmosphere will soften edges and lessen contrasts, making objects appear less distinct as the distance increases.

When I pull farther away from God, His size, importance, and abilities seem smaller. As my perception of Him diminishes, the less aware I become of Him and the less power I give Him. But when I draw in close, when I approach Him—whether boldly and confidently or with humility and reverence—He becomes magnified. The air crackles with power. The atmosphere warms. And, confronted with the enormity and power of our mighty God, I realize that He can make a difference. My awe increases as His presence becomes tangible. It's impossible to breathe without Him. He fills my mind and thoughts and vision. He becomes everything to me. When we use perspective as a way to look at God, He ceases to be flat and lifeless and becomes more real than we ever imagined.

He becomes our reality. One we can no longer dispute.

But, even after experiencing Him in this way, sometimes I turn my back on Him. I decide He can wait until after I fix dinner, pick up the twelve pairs of shoes scattered around the back door, run to the bank. It doesn't take long before I realize I'm not living in His shadow anymore—and, irrational or not, I might blame Him for moving away. He didn't abandon *me*, though; it's the other way around.

Note that God's *actual* size and power and willingness and presence never change. It's our perspective, our relationship to Him that does. We choose what we see by selecting where we stand.

> When I pull farther away from God, His size, importance, and abilities seem smaller. But when I draw in close, He becomes magnified. He becomes everything to me.

A Change of Perspective

Your particular view of a situation can provide the empathy you need to fervently pray for someone else. In chapter 7, I recounted an experience I had with an abusive man and how my prayers have changed as a result. That experience was the impetus I needed to pray for a friend of mine who spent years married to that man. When I put myself in her shoes, I now pray for her healing and his, along with my own. My prayer has become exponentially magnified.

My friend Heather wrote on her blog, "Perspective isn't this static thing. It's not a feeling. It's not an emotional state. It's not the way you view things. It's the way you *see* them. There is only one way to make what you see in front of you different. You have to get up. Up from where you planted yourself. You have to stand up and move to another spot."[20] When you do that, the objects don't change, but your view of them will.

It's imperative that you keep your position steady when you draw from life, because the slightest shift in location changes the angle of perspective and the shapes of the spaces between objects. You will only see the exact view another person sees if you are standing in an identical position. If you're drawing a still life, and you take a break and come back to it, you can't slouch if you were sitting tall before. You can't scoot your drawing board to the right to make room for a cup of coffee. A shorter person who sits in your seat will not see the same things from there, because even those slight movements change the point of view.

But in prayer, sometimes you want a different perspective. No matter what you do, you're convinced God is wearing prayer-canceling headphones, because if He could hear you, you are certain He would answer. And He hasn't. You've prayed the same thing so long that you've run out of ways to say it—until even *you* no longer feel the passion behind the words.

In prayer, sometimes you want a different perspective. You've prayed the same thing so long that you've run out of ways to say it—until even you *no longer feel the passion behind the words.*

Early in their marriage, Nathan and Peggy moved into the basement of his parents' house. Peggy was struggling with moving back to a small town from Indianapolis, with no longer being defined by the career she gave up for motherhood, and with seeing the writing on the wall that her husband was headed down the path that would lead to them stepping into ministry. She felt like they had lost all the forward movement they'd gained in their adult lives and were lower than where they'd begun. Nathan was working hard to get them out of debt, to get them on their feet again. Her toddler was bouncing off the walls, and the low basement ceiling seemed to be an impenetrable barrier, keeping her prayers from going up and keeping God from coming down.

As Peggy talked about this to Ann, an elder in the church, Ann offered a solution: She'd pray for Peggy and her family's needs. Her only condition was that Peggy stop praying for herself. Just stop.

Instead, she should pick out someone in the church and pray that God would answer *that person's* prayers—and let Ann carry Peggy's prayer burdens for a while.

Peggy's first instinct was to pray that Ann's prayers would be answered, but she knew that wasn't the point. Peggy trusted that Ann would be true to her word and that her own prayer needs wouldn't be neglected, so she was able to put down her burdens and lift up someone else's. The change in perspective released Peggy from her dark cave and allowed her to see God again, to feel Him, to believe He was still involved and active. Before long, both women saw their prayers answered.

This example is just another way to pray upside down. Flip-flop your needs with a friend's—or drop your own load to free you to carry someone else's. No money? Give something away to change your perspective. (*I may be poor, but I still have more than I need.*) Did you lose your job? Don't sit around depressed. Instead, fill your days: Help an elderly neighbor do yard work, offer to lead that week's Sunday school class to give the teacher a break, and find blessings in your newfound free time.

> *Flip-flop your needs with a friend's—or drop your own load to free you to carry someone else's.*

Update your résumé. Volunteer to grade spelling tests in your child's classroom. Have a job that you hate? Brighten your outlook: Take a coworker to coffee to cheer her up, find a way to genuinely compliment your boss, volunteer for a task that seems overwhelming to someone else, or pick flowers from your yard to brighten the reception desk.

Anything you do to provide an alternate viewpoint helps you see the situation differently. It may still be a job you don't like, but now you have a better friend. Or a newfound sympathy for your boss's burdens. Or simply a little vase full of color when you walk in the door. When you look at your situation from a different angle, you just might be able to see God where He seemed to be hiding before.

Two Points of View—From the Same Position

We can complain because rose bushes have thorns,
or rejoice because thorn bushes have roses.

ATTRIBUTED TO ABRAHAM LINCOLN

Most of the time, whatever situation you're in, there are multiple ways to look at it. Which one you choose matters and can change your outlook dramatically. As tennis legend John McEnroe put it, perception is everything. "There are two ways to look at it: 'Wow, I won seven majors,' or 'Man, I didn't win a major after 25, whatta loser.'"[21]

Sometimes seeing the bad can help define the good. This is why, when our kids were younger, they loved it when we'd declare it Rude Night. This was a special meal during which they could indulge in every bit of rude behavior they could think of—belching loudly, reaching in front of someone for the salt, eating off their plates like a dog, or throwing food (as long as it was gently tossed to someone else, not splattered against the walls or smooshed into the carpet). They had a blast—and you know what? It taught them as much as if we had been uptight about the rules. They had to know what good behavior was in order to distinguish the bad.

If you think about it, you'll see examples all over the place of something unexpectedly good that comes from something that, on the surface, appears bad (or at least less than ideal).

If you think about it, you'll see examples all over the place of something unexpectedly good that comes from something that, on the surface, appears bad (or at least less than ideal). Penicillin comes from mold. Rotting grapes turn into wine. Labor pains result in the presence of a long-awaited child. I rarely see the inside of a gym, but I know that the sweat and discomfort of exercise bring about better health. If you just watch for it, you'll find God in the middle of some surprising things.

In 2012, Indiana—and much of the country—suffered a drought. Lawns crunched underfoot, the grass dry and brown, just like the acres of farmland my sister and I inherited when my mom passed away. The farm manager, Bill, kept calling with bad news. I'd been praying for rain, praying that somehow the crops wouldn't be as bad as we expected, that the farmers would make enough money to survive for another year, and that we would have a little bit of profit too. The rain finally came—weeks too late to make a difference. The plants' roots were dead, and they couldn't soak up any of the water. Instead, the brittle cornstalks folded under the weight of the water hitting them.

To make matters worse, we got hit by a hailstorm. I tried not to be ungrateful, but really? Not exactly an answer to my prayers.

Bill called one day to say that one of the farms only yielded six bushels of corn per acre (compared to around 190 bushels in previous years). The soybeans were still a loss, but we had hail damage insurance on the corn, so we would be getting a check from the insurance company. It only gave us about half of what we would have earned, had it been a good year. But a lot more than we would have gotten if the hail had missed us.

In other words, thank God for the hail! It wasn't God hitting us when we were down. It was God's upside-down way of answering our prayers. As usual, it wasn't the answer we expected. And as always, it was just what we needed.

Too often, we miss seeing God because we think His answer will look different than it does. The dream job you don't get, six months before the company goes belly-up, flooding the work-force with hundreds more job applicants. The train stopped on the tracks, making you late for an appointment, but keeping you well out of reach of the drunk driver weaving across the road. Some of these things, like the hailstorm, we are lucky enough to see. Some we don't. When you can't see the good, when it looks like God isn't listening or He's not giving you your heart's desires, remember the storm that redeemed our harvest. Even if it doesn't always make sense, uncurl your clenched fists and instead extend your hands in praise—and thank God for the hail.

Because sometimes, against all logic, the best answer is another storm.

PRAYER PALETTE

My eyesight may be getting weaker, but my vision is increasing.
~J. C. PENNEY

I'LL PRAY FOR YOU IF YOU PRAY FOR ME. Trade requests with a trusted friend, and devote time every day to lifting up that need to God on your friend's behalf. If your request is private and you don't want to reveal details but still want prayer, you may write it on a piece of paper (or simply write the word *unspoken*), seal it in an envelope, and let your friend use the envelope as a visual reminder to pray.

CHANGE POSITIONS. One way to shift your perspective is to examine a situation through someone else's eyes. Different people notice different things and solve problems in their own unique ways. For example, if you were able to sit across the table from Steve Jobs, who was known for his innovation of Apple products and ways of solving needs we didn't even know we had, how might he approach the problem? What would Maya Angelou have suggested? How would Mother Teresa view the issue? What questions would Einstein ask? How would Walt Disney have completed the story? (Or Dr. Seuss?) What solutions might the president of the United States propose? Your grandfather? Your younger self? The person on the other end of your need (your spouse, boss, child, friend)?

Write down your prayer; then list six or eight influential people beneath that. Choose one or two, and then write the prayer as you imagine that person would pray it (whether or not that person is actually one who prays—just pretend). Stay open to insights that come from that different perspective.

Copying an image is easier using the grid method.

CHAPTER 11

BREAKING IT INTO MANAGEABLE PIECES

(THE GRID METHOD)

---

*Trouble and perplexity drive me to prayer, and
prayer drives away perplexity and trouble.*

PHILIP MELANCHTHON

Toni, like most moms, was overwhelmed by all that she needed to do. All those trivial things stayed on her radar, distracting her from the important things. So she did what my friend Lisa calls a "brain dump." She got a fresh legal pad and started making a master to-do list, giving herself permission to let go of each item once she wrote it down, no longer reserving space in her over-cluttered brain since there was now a record elsewhere. She wrote and wrote until the pad was filled and her mind was emptied. (FYI, my list would look like this: *Call about the rebate we should have received. Return those shoes to Target. Get estimates to replace broken window on the back porch. Call AT&T about upgrading data plan. Update expired credit card information with PayPal. Reschedule mammogram.* And that's just for starters.)

After examining her list, Toni asked herself what mattered to her the most. Only two things remained: (1) Be a mom, and (2) Write. Without all the clutter bogging her down, she found her focus. And it seems to have worked for her: Novelist Toni Morrison has written eight novels, won the Nobel Prize for Literature, the Pulitzer Prize, and the Presidential Medal of Freedom. As a single mother, she raised her two sons alongside her successful writing career.[22]

When there is a big project in front of us (or a lot of little ones), sometimes we don't know where to begin. The myriad tasks, eventualities, and considerations may paralyze us, keeping us from beginning. It can be the same with art. Drawing a bowl of fruit on a smooth tabletop—okay, I can probably handle that. Crafting a composition as elaborate as Michelangelo's masterpiece on the ceiling of the Sistine Chapel—well, where do you even begin? At the center of the action, where God's hand is outstretched to Adam? What if you have your scale wrong and you run out of room for part of the painting?

I've heard that Michelangelo started at the edges and worked his way in, knowing he would be a better painter once he reached the critical center. I would have started at the middle to make sure I included the most important part. Even the great masters create sometimes out of their comfort zones—after all, Michelangelo was primarily a sculptor, not a painter. But that didn't stop him from tackling this project.

Sometimes a composition is too complex, the perspective too challenging, or the details too daunting. At times like these, an artist will employ the grid method, which is a way to copy an image by overlaying it with a grid of equal-sized squares. On the final canvas, the artist makes a second grid (typically larger), then copies the original one square at a time, paying attention to the places where objects cross the edges of the squares as a way of keeping the rendering accurate and in proportion.

Usually, this method is employed to transfer a sketch for a large wall mural from a piece of paper. Without it, the composition could become skewed, the proportions off. But there are also beginning artists who use this method as they're learning to draw, when copying a portrait, for instance. It's not a way to create something new but to help reproduce what you can already see.

Breaking Down

When my daughter Katie entered high school, she also entered the world of migraine sufferers. She was enrolled in summer PE, and she kept waking up with excruciating headaches. (I've since learned that there is a big difference between a headache and a migraine; she was having migraines.) After a few weeks, her teacher called to say that Katie would fail if she didn't drop the class because she wasn't earning her participation grade. While the thought of PE might have caused me to have a migraine, Katie wasn't trying to get out of it. She was truly suffering.

And that was just the beginning. Over the next three years,

we consulted allergists, family practitioners, and neurologists, trying various combinations and classes of medications to prevent and/or stop the migraines. Early in the first semester of her senior year, the meds struck a truce with the migraines, keeping them at bay. But then, because of unwanted interactions between two of the drugs, we changed one of her meds, and the peace treaty devolved into all-out war. Katie woke up with a migraine every day for two weeks, swallowed a pill with her eyes squeezed tight against the light, and burrowed back under the covers.

I left message after message with the vice principal in charge of attendance. "Hi. Me again." I left voice mails for the neurologist's nurse, begging her to call me back to discuss how to get some relief for Katie. I called the doctor who prescribed the new meds and convinced her Katie should stop taking them. I scheduled follow-up appointments. And I checked and rechecked Katie's grades online, e-mailing her teachers to ask for extensions and convince them she wasn't faking it.

I tried to sympathize with my daughter, knowing she couldn't will the headaches away, but she could hear my frustration. I defended Katie to well-meaning friends and family—including her dad—who questioned the validity of each headache. I did everything I could think of, but I couldn't escape the worry. After sleeping all day in the dark, once the medicines took effect, Katie was better—so every evening, she sat in the living room watching a Lifetime movie and looking just fine. "Katie, shouldn't you be reading? Katie, have you done your chemistry yet?" Her whining about her head grated on my nerves. My nagging grated on hers. She was grumpy and worn out (from what we call migraine hangovers). And I was so tired of trying to carry it all for her.

Finally, after Katie had missed two weeks of school, I took her to the ER and they gave her IV meds that kicked the migraines—for the moment. When I eventually met with the vice principal face-to-face, the overachiever in me took a deep breath and cut Katie's schedule in half, hoping that starting later would give the meds time to knock out her daily headaches before she had to be at school. We crossed our fingers, hoping that the college she was planning to attend next year wouldn't mind the schedule changes or rescind her scholarships. Suddenly, we were counseling our honors student about the strategy of just trying to complete half—because a couple of 50 percent grades are easier to recover from than zeros.

It's never fun being a parent when your child is having problems, whatever they are. But we do what we have to do. And there is never a good time to have issues that require a lot of time and attention. But during these two weeks, I had a rare three-day business trip and a flood of new work. My fifth-grade son had just revealed that a diorama related to a Newbery Medal book he hadn't yet read was due in three days. I had to compile tax information for my accountant in order to meet the financial aid deadline, because without it (and assuming her migraines didn't keep her from graduating), Katie wouldn't receive her scholarships the next year. My dad needed a mailing sent out for his upcoming workshop, and my pastor had just received information about the conference our church was hosting in three weeks. The flyers needed to go out two weeks ago. Or, at the latest, today. I jumped through hoops to meet my clients' unreasonable deadlines so we could pay the stack of bills for Katie's various tests, prescriptions, and procedures. The rest of my family needed to go to practices, wear clean clothes, and have an occasional meal. My husband wondered if I'd ever watch TV with him again. And all the while, Katie's migraines got worse, not better.

I was too overwhelmed to pray. Too tired, too frustrated. It was all too much.

Breaking It Down

I took a step back. I knew God could handle it all, even if I couldn't (perhaps *especially* since I couldn't). I had to find a way to break down my worries into smaller, more manageable parts to begin to cope. To keep things in the proper perspective. It's how I solve most of my scheduling issues, the ones not obliterated by Karin's Sharpie—by addressing one thing at a time. I put everything on the calendar, down to the tiniest details. *Buy cleaning supplies on Monday. Run to the post office on Tuesday between 9 and 9:15. Get prescription refills on Thursdays because I'll be on that side of town for Bible study.* I set alerts on my phone to help me remember dentist and hair appointments. I ordered lots of pizzas.

But the issues I faced with Katie weren't things I could fix by scheduling—or by making lists or hundreds of phone calls. I did what I hate to admit I often do. I waited until the problems consumed me completely before asking God to help. By that point, I didn't have a clue where to start in prayer.

So I prayed about it one square at a time.

I said, *God, You know it all. I need You to be in all of this. But for today, all I can think about are Katie's grades. Please help.*

But it wasn't easy. I kept having to reel myself in because, before I knew it, I'd give in to the flood of worry threatening to drown me. I kept getting stuck ruminating on the potential ramifications—looking at the whole grid—and wondering how in the world I could fix these problems.

The short answer is that I couldn't. Neither can you. But God can.

Months earlier, we'd heard about a migraine specialty clinic three hours from home. I'd promised Katie she could pick a trip to anywhere in the continental United States for her senior year, and she finally chose—the hospital in Chicago. We packed and made arrangements to be gone, but the doctors at the clinic decided at her pre-admission appointment that hospitalization wasn't necessary. So her big trip consisted of one night out of town, a couple of new meds, and an impromptu trip to IKEA, which made me happy but didn't do a thing for Katie's pain.

But after several more months of suffering, when the migraines were measured in weeks, not days, and the attendance officer recognized my voice, the clinic decided to admit her. Of course, spring break was past. I couldn't make arrangements for care for my other kids on such short notice, and my husband couldn't get time off work, so my only choice was to leave Katie at the hospital alone. Her condition wasn't life threatening. She was bright and capable. But I cried like a baby as I rode the elevator down to the parking garage and drove home. She was eighteen, but still *my* baby, and I couldn't do anything except pray. I couldn't even commiserate with my mom, because she was gone.

A week later, things began falling into place. I brought Katie home, pain-free for the first time in months. Without a throbbing head, alone in her hospital room, she had nearly caught up with her homework. And she was in a much better mood, so I was too. She'd missed senior awards night but retained her scholarships. Finals were two weeks away, and she was well enough to attend the review sessions. Three weeks later, she graduated, headache-free, with one B+ and the rest As. And all those little worries, the day-to-day details? We somehow took care of what was important; my family never missed a meal, my projects were completed on time, and we paid the final bill for her hospital stay as Katie packed for college.

> *If we can pray, then we can connect with God. It's that simple. God sees it all, and I believe He continues to answer even if we don't know what to ask for.*

Praying with the grid method doesn't necessarily change the way God answers. But having a way to simplify these convoluted, complex situations helps *us*, because it enables us to pray, rather than curling up in a ball in the corner in complete emotional overload. If we can pray, then we can connect with God. It's that simple. If we can grasp one little square, He will lift the others.

When you're stuck, you don't have to pick one "right" thing. God sees it all, and I believe He continues to answer even if we don't know what to ask for. Because, really, how *can* we know? The answer to the bills you can't pay might be more money. Or fewer cable channels. It may be that you need a new job that offers opportunity for advancement, a reasonable budget plan, or that you need to learn how to go to Target without emptying your bank account. It may cost you more initially—maybe you need to attend college to land a better-paying career. You may need to focus on your health because the medical bills for specialists, tests, facilities, anesthesiologists, and procedures are piling up—or an answer might be stumbling upon a new client whose projects help cover the bills. You may need to walk away from clients who pay slowly (if at all) or from your existing clients who might need a business boost. You may need to go back to work with a company that offers better health insurance benefits.

My point is simple: We don't always know the best way through a problem. Because there are so many possible ways, and direction isn't always easy to find.

Unfortunately, even when we think a problem is solved, it might not really be over. God responded to my plea for help with Katie's health issues, grades, and medical bills, but as I revise this chapter, we need help again. Two years later, Katie is now a sophomore in college. The frequency and magnitude of her headaches have ratcheted up again, and the side effects require a change of drugs. She's twenty, so she has taken charge of her medical care, and she called me a couple of weeks ago to tell me they were admitting her to the hospital again.

"But you have class!"

"I haven't been to class for two weeks because I've had migraines every day."

"Oh." I'm still unable to help. She's still hurting. This time she drove four hours to the hospital—all by herself. I cried from the comfort of my own home.

They kept her five days, as planned—and then four more. She had problems with her IVs and had to have a PICC line. This time the headaches didn't cease completely, so she's back at school, rearranging her schedule, realizing she might have to retake some of the classes—one professor even encouraging her to drop out of college until she is healthy again. Keeping her scholarships isn't the top priority anymore. She may have to let them go. Now her challenge is learning to live and function with the migraines.

In the meantime, our seventeen-year-old daughter, Anna—a swimmer—needs a second shoulder surgery, and my husband was told, as he was locking up his workplace on New Year's Eve, that he was being let go, effective immediately, because of corporate restructuring. Three months later, he's still home. Which is actually a good thing, because my graphic design business is experiencing levels of success previously known only in dreams (scary ones), and I need his help at home. Taxes and financial aid deadlines are here—again—always a rough time for me as a small business owner who doesn't have time (or the necessary discipline) for all that paperwork.

And my dad was just diagnosed with cancer, less than three years after Mom succumbed to it. During his ongoing treatment for high-grade dysplasia, they found cancer, deeper and more extensive than they had imagined. As I write, we don't have all the biopsies back. We have more questions than answers and a hard road ahead of us.

I thought I was handling the news okay—until Sunday morning, as I stood in my usual spot at church, eyes closed, trying to sing a worship song, when my guard fell completely. The thought that consumed me wasn't one of grief or anger, but surprise. *I can't believe I'm back here again.*

I want to do it better this time. I want to lean in to God, not shove Him aside. I want to bring His strength into all of our lives. I want to stop myself from building another thick, impenetrable wall to keep me from feeling. And this is how I know grace: God is not mad at me for not staying strong when I lost my mom. He's not annoyed that Katie's migraines are back with a vengeance or that we need His help again. He's holding out His arms, stepping past the sloppy base layers of stone I'm trying to erect around me, saying, "Stay with Me. You don't have to carry all of this. You don't have to solve it. Let Me do it this time."

In Matthew 9:1-2, some people brought a paralyzed man to Jesus. His first words? "Be encouraged, my child! Your sins are forgiven." It seems that He didn't take care of the obvious issue first, the man's paralysis. But actually, Jesus went straight to the thing that mattered the most. And then, only then, did He heal the man. Over and over, Jesus flips the world's ideas on their heads.

One little square may just hint at a whole picture. But our God sees it—and way beyond. His role is to draw in the missing pieces, finish the puzzle, make the connections, and put things together right. Ours is to pick one square, any square, and hold it up to Him in prayer. He wants us to ask for help. Needs come—and they go—and there's *always* something more that I can bring to God's feet with a humble request (or desperate plea) for help. He waits for me, every day. He hopes I'll show up.

Just hold up one piece of the grid. Believe that He has hold of the other side and that He's working on more than you see. Pray, and watch eagerly as the picture takes shape.

One square at a time.

PRAYER PALETTE

To see things simply is the hardest thing in the world.
~CHARLES HAWTHORNE, HAWTHORNE ON PAINTING

PRAY FOR THE COLOR BLUE. When my kids were young, cleaning their rooms was an intimidating task, until I made a list. First, I told them to pick up everything blue and put it where it belonged. Then yellow items, purple, green, and the list continues. As they got older, I'd suggest that they start by throwing away the trash. Put dirty clothes in the laundry room. Books on shelves. Clean clothes in drawers. One thing, one category, at a time. Eventually, what seems overwhelming becomes manageable.

To apply this to prayer, keep it simple: Pray for every person you see today wearing the color green (or white, or red). Or make a list of concepts, and every day, choose one as a prayer focus. The list might contain categories such as strangers, teachers, pastors, those who are sick, marriages, friendship, employers, children, doctors, local businesses, individual churches in your community, national figures. As you are standing in line at the grocery store or waiting at the airport, scroll through your contacts and pray for anyone whose name catches your eye.

PRAY THROUGH THE ALPHABET. Down the left-hand side of a sheet of paper, write the alphabet. Fill in the first person, place, or situation that comes to mind that starts with each letter. As you write, pray for that. A: Anna *(Help her stop stressing about her college decision, heal her shoulder)*. B: Busy *(Lord, show me how to be less busy, how to take on only the things that are good for my family and honor you)*.

The pencil sketch and the finished watercolor are two different approaches to the same subject.

CHAPTER 12

DEVELOPING YOUR SKILLS

(SKETCHING AND DRAWING)

Art is a collaboration between God and the artist,
and the less the artist does the better.

ANDRÉ GIDE

When I first began attending Grace & Mercy and started to explore prayer, my friend Tami told me about a particularly trying time in her life. She was having financial difficulties and struggles with her stepchildren. I was worried for her and didn't know how to make it better.

A few days later she told me things were looking up.

"What happened?" I asked.

"Oh," she said. "I put on worship music last night and prayed for a couple of hours, and now I just feel really good about everything."

I nodded, acting like, *Oh, of course. Sure.* But my mind started spinning, playing the conversation over and over, because I really didn't understand what in the world she was talking about. As soon as Tami left, I turned on the iron to tackle a pile of wrinkled clothes, and I did that thing where you talk/pray/gripe in your head to yourself and/or God. (Or maybe I'm the only one who does that.) I was mad, annoyed, frustrated. Troubled by a concept I'd never considered.

I don't get it. Two hours? Who has two extra hours in a day? What in the world did she have to say? How on earth would that be helpful? Doesn't God already know everything? I mean, don't You, Lord?

I'll never forget that moment. It was one of the first times I heard from God. As soon as I'd formed the questions in my mind, the answer popped into my head, crystal clear.

"You already know what Katie does at school, but you want to hear it from her."

That was the year that my oldest daughter started kindergarten, and even though I knew more or less what she experienced each day, I couldn't wait until she came home and would tell me all about it. In her words, from her perspective. In detail.

I'd already visited the classroom and felt good about her teacher. I saw the worksheets that came home in her backpack, so I knew what they'd learned that day. I didn't really need to know if they had goldfish crackers or Oreos for snack time. It wasn't important whether they'd read Dr. Seuss or Shel Silverstein in story time; nor did it matter whether their teacher or the librarian read to them. I didn't necessarily need to know that she finished her worksheet before Jacob or that her blue crayon broke.

But because I loved her and was invested in her growth, I delighted in hearing her quirky observations. The things she noticed told me what mattered to her. The people she talked about were the ones who would shape her and help her grow. As a parent, I was providing her with the opportunities to have, and process, new experiences. As she talked, they became mine—ours—not just hers. The stories became part of our shared palette of experience.

A sketch is generally more spirited than a picture. It is the artist's work when he is full of inspiration and ardour, when reflection has toned down nothing, it is the artist's soul expressing itself freely on the canvas.

DENIS DIDEROT, *DIDEROT'S THOUGHTS ON ART & STYLE*

When an artist does a sketch, he is trying to express the general idea, representing the object or idea at its most basic level. Sometimes there is great passion and power in the emotion of the moment. Sketching expresses a concept quickly and communicates what is essential. If you're at all like me, you may find yourself doing lots of sketching in your prayer life.

Sound familiar? *I want to pray, but I need to fold the laundry before it wrinkles and pick up milk before the kids get home,* or *I'll wait until the mail comes,* or *I would pray now but my computer just dinged with the arrival of three new e-mails. And look at that—it's already time to go to the ball game.* I'd rather pray quickly than not at all, so I do my version of a prayer sketch. *Lord, heal her. Forgive me. Touch him. Fix this. Help me know what to do. Thank You.*

Time isn't always the issue; sometimes it's a lack of words. You're overwhelmed, scared, weary, distant, and you want God. But all you can do is whisper one or two desperate words. *Help.* Or *Lord, I have no words, but I know You know.* . . . There's something to be said for the bare, honest truth. For laying out the core of your desires or needs in the most basic, least embellished fashion. These prayers aren't always pretty, but they are expressive and passionate and legitimate. I've seen hundreds of these simple requests answered quickly and powerfully.

Sketching expresses a concept quickly and communicates what is essential. If you're at all like me, you may find yourself doing lots of sketching in your prayer life.

I'm so grateful that the power of my prayers isn't based on how well I say them, but on the power of the One who hears them.

Okay, so if God answers desperate, succinct prayers (and brief, grateful, happy prayers), why bother with anything else?

Sketching (in art) is a way of honing your observational skills or planning a more complicated piece. It's a method of teaching your hand to follow your eyes. It might be used to work out a complicated detail, explore an idea, determine the best composition, or just serve as a visual "note to self." In most cases, the sketch is the first step, the starting point from which deeper, more complex art can emerge. Sketches are valuable as tools, and some sketches by masterful artists are prized as art objects because they show us the thought process of the artist. (Or sometimes simply because they're beautiful.)

While artists understand the value and beauty of sketching, they rarely stop there. The majority of the walls in art museums hold elaborate, intricate, carefully wrought paintings and drawings. These pieces required time, talent, and focus—a deeper commitment and serious discipline. Not everyone can be a master artist, just as not everyone will have the inclination or interest to pray in great depth. But there is a difference between making a quick sketch and rendering something in great detail. This difference applies to prayer as well.

When an artist studies an object in order to do a detailed drawing or painting, he learns more about the object than he knew before. Sir Kenneth Clark wrote, "It is often said that Leonardo [da Vinci] drew so well because he knew about things; it is truer to say that he knew about things because he drew so well."[23] While I think both viewpoints contain truth, I know that an artist has to see the nuances in order to render a subject in exquisite detail. He may notice the way the light shapes the curve of the apple, the glare of the silver bowl's reflection, the variation of textures. He will recognize the relationships between the objects and the way the colors reflecting off one item change the highlights on another. His quick sketch might be beautiful, and it might accurately represent the scene on the table. But it likely won't reveal every detail. It won't have you longing to reach out and touch it, wanting to bite into the ripe red fruit, already imagining the way the juice will dribble down your chin as you eat.

Our prayers might be answered when we pray quickly and simply—in fact, many of them will. Prayer sketches are a valuable, concise way to communicate with God. But a part of me isn't fully satisfied with the quick, easy approach. I yearn to truly connect, to find the beauty in quiet contemplation. To develop a sense of companionship, to let my relationship with God mature. No matter how much you sketch or pray, there is always the opportunity to go deeper. This is available to me—and to you—whenever we want it, whenever we approach our unfathomable, endless, timeless God.

At times, I am easily distracted and quick to be consumed with petty, ungodly emotions (the drawing equivalent of big, ugly scribbles). Sometimes I don't feel like going deep. And other times

I don't feel capable of anything more than a quick prayer. So I send up quick thoughts throughout my days, and when I can find or make time to really focus, I do.

If you're the same way, wanting what you can't always find, take comfort in knowing that not every piece Michelangelo created was a masterpiece. He didn't become a master overnight, and no matter how many exquisite pieces he crafted, he never stopped sketching. The more you sketch, the better you will draw. Most artists suggest drawing something every day until it becomes second nature, so that what your eye sees, your hand draws. Whether or not you ever become a great artist, you can still work toward the prayer equivalent.

Turning your quick sketch into a detailed drawing requires spending time reflecting, talking, *and* listening. It comes from desire and requires spending time in the white space—just *being* with Him. Going deep doesn't require an aptitude for putting together eloquent, flowery words.

Those words are available to you, even if they weren't originally yours. If you feel out of your element, and your soul craves beautifully crafted words, there are plenty to explore. It's a completely legitimate way to pray and can yield tremendous benefits. Read the Bible or explore poetry or liturgy; their essences are like a flawlessly executed painting. Years ago, men and women of faith spent hours, days, even weeks crafting each prayer. They incorporated Scripture, carefully selecting each and every word. They searched deep in their souls with intention, looking for beauty, truth, and power.

Those things are yours for the asking. Just start exploring.

❋ ❋ ❋

During a writing workshop I attended, a well-known author assigned us the task of sitting for thirty minutes in three very different locations and writing down every single detail we observed. That evening, after we shared our notes with each other, she told us that they now belonged to us all. What the other women observed became part of my repertoire, and my observations became part of theirs. Because we shared, I can now absorb the ideas, make them part of my story, and weave them into the fabric of who I am.

Have you ever noticed that at family reunions or book club gatherings, the same stories surface time and time again? Everyone laughs (or cries or wonders or rejoices or tries to puzzle it out so it makes sense) every time. I believe this is because God made us for relationships, and shared experiences connect us. When we replay these events together, our bonds are strengthened. The stories belong to everyone in them and to those who are part of the retelling.

What God showed me that morning as I stood at the ironing board forever changed my understanding of prayer. What I wanted to hear from Katie is exactly what I think God wants to hear from us when we pray: observations, discussions, thoughts, questions. When we share our moments with God in detail, they cease to belong only to us. When we describe a problem to Him, in the process we will inevitably grasp a new facet of His character and discern new perspectives. Even if God's answer to the sketch prayer is exactly the same as the result of the in-depth one (because, let's face it—whether we tell Him the details or not, He knows them), *we* will be changed. Because we've entered into relationship. It's the difference between the quick gesture and the detailed, careful rendering. Both are good and both are valuable.

> *Jesus came to experience life* with *us. Isn't that what you and I long for? To share this life with Him?*

But the one that requires more effort potentially yields a different kind of insight.

Besides, isn't that why Jesus came? To experience life *with* us? And isn't that what you and I long for? To share this life with Him? Jesus taught through parables, knowing the inherent value in telling stories. I think He loves it when we tell ours back to Him.

* * *

Remember the day my friend Tami prayed? The challenges of blending two families didn't immediately cease. Bills were still due and tensions were still high at home. But when she spent time with God, she found comfort in not being alone. She shared her feelings and knew He understood. Gradually, her frustrations were replaced by gratitude for the little ones in her care and clarity about how to live in the role she'd been given. Tami came to know, from a place deep within her, that—together, with God—she would get through this, and in due time she would even forget these problems. Her answers weren't momentous, and they weren't broadcast on the five o'clock news. But by spending time with God talking it out, she began to grasp the first steps she needed to take. She learned to explain financial realities and value differences to the kids so that they didn't have unrealistic expectations. She learned to be open with her husband about her frustrations so she wasn't carrying all the weight by herself. And she learned that God cared about every single little detail.

> "That is why I tell you not to worry about everyday life—
> whether you have enough food and drink, or enough
> clothes to wear. . . . Can all your worries add a single
> moment to your life?" [Jesus asked.] "Your heavenly
> Father already knows all your needs. Seek the Kingdom of

God above all else, and live righteously, and he will give you everything you need."

MATTHEW 6:25, 27, 32-33

Seems backwards, doesn't it? By not worrying about the details, you'll find everything you need? In believing this, Tami found joy. Not happiness, which can be fleeting. She wasn't pleased to be facing her problems, but she grabbed hold of the inexplicable joy that can be found—whatever hurdle or worry or sadness or trouble you're facing—when you allow God to walk beside you as you go through it.

As for me, I'm still learning. I'd call myself an apprentice more than a master. But on that day, Tami inspired me to reach for more. She effectively sketched for me a picture of the detailed, carefully articulated relationship I wanted to find. A thing of enduring beauty.

A true work of art.

PRAYER PALETTE

A work of art is finished from the point of view of the artist, when feeling and perception have resulted in a spiritual synthesis.
~HANS HOFMANN

BRIEF SKETCHES. If you spend dedicated time in prayer but don't pray except when all other activity has ceased, or if you often forget to pray at all, put Post-it notes or index cards on the fridge and by light switches as reminders. Change your computer password to a prompt—DontForget2Pray, Pray24/7.[24] Set a daily reminder on your phone at a time when you can typically take a few moments to pray. Write with dry-erase markers on your mirrors or on plain fridge magnets. Respond to these reminders by sending up a quick prayer sketch as you walk out the door, as you brush your teeth, as you load the dishwasher.

WORK ON YOUR CRAFT. Artists improve their skills only through practice, by dedicating time to their work. Apply this idea to prayer by setting aside time to try different things.

- Experiment with locations (in your house, in the car, taking a walk, sitting on the porch) and times of day. (Are early mornings peaceful and uninterrupted time for you, or are you most focused midday or late at night when everyone else is asleep?)

- How do different positions enhance or detract from your prayer experience? Try sitting, kneeling, walking, bowing your head, clasping your hands together, lying facedown, standing with arms raised, dancing.

- Does music help you focus, or does it distract you? Does listening to old hymns, gospel, contemporary rock, or mainstream pop make you feel more spiritual?

- Does reading the Bible or a devotional book direct your thoughts toward God? Does reciting a written prayer allow you to start the flow of your own words?

Take notes about your experiences. Before long, you'll find your own style—and maybe discover something entirely new.

Sketching allows an artist to quickly explore multiple directions.

CHAPTER 13

THE IMPORTANCE OF THE PROCESS

(KEEPING A SKETCHBOOK)

---

*A man's work is nothing but this slow trek to rediscover,
through the detours of art, those two or three great and
simple images in whose presence his heart first opened.*

ALBERT CAMUS, *LYRICAL AND CRITICAL ESSAYS*

Confession time: I've always envied those folks with a flair for fashion, who can wear things like tortoiseshell glasses and vintage aprons over jeans and somehow look incomparably cool. (Yes, Kelly B., I mean you!) That kind of style doesn't come naturally to me. In college, I had to make a concerted effort to look like an art student—buy black boots and purposely shop for trench coats at thrift stores, for example. Until then, I didn't know there was such a thing as a thrift store.

Even more than their sense of style, I envied the sketchbooks the older art majors (the painters and sculptors) carried, big black books whose covers had been turned into veritable works of art. To me, this was proof of the owner's legitimacy—*this person*, the book declared, *is an artist.*

Because I'm a dork and wanted to be one of them, I traded my usual spiral-bound sketchbook for a thick, hardbound book filled with creamy white pages. And then I pored over magazines (mainly *Rolling Stone* and *Architectural Digest*) to clip beautiful designs, punny headlines, colorful shapes and quotes, copies of da Vinci's sketches, and the prism from the Pink Floyd album *The Dark Side of the Moon*. I layered, hand-drew letters, colored, cut, and glued, wrapping it all with a clear plastic laminate when I was done.

See? I'm a real artist, I thought.

I filled page after page of that sketchbook with logo sketches for a class project (ten pages of exploring the letter *A* in a bazillion fonts, sizes, relationships, positions). Designing a travel brochure allowed me to pull out my grandfather's stamp collection, carefully copying foreign stamps and playing with accordion-folding techniques (like a road map, only less maddening). A senior honors thesis on corporate identity gave me the opportunity to name an imaginary Kaleidoscope Children's Museum, research stained-glass patterns, and sketch children in different poses and styles for the logo. I colored patterns, noting how placement of colors changed the overall effect—for instance, if the shapes were blue on a green background or if they were green on a blue background.

Having the sketchbook didn't require me to do any extra work. These steps were part of the process of completing each project. But it gave me permission to play. I learned the value of recording what I found, creating a treasure trove of inspiration, and making a visual record. It didn't take long for me to fall in love with the work that the sketchbook represented. The finished projects that had to be carefully rendered and neatly spray-mounted onto crisp black boards—well, those weren't as fun, but they were necessary for grades. But the process. Oh, wow, the process.

Within a few years, I earned a bachelor of fine arts degree with honors, but not because of the paisley jeans, black boots, and trench coats. I'll be honest, it didn't happen because my sketchbook cover was so pretty or all of my projects were exceptional. It was because of what I learned about the value of the process.

I'll never forget my first interview for a graphic design internship. At a prestigious Indianapolis ad agency, four art directors gathered around my portfolio, gaping at me, shocked that I could explain the strategic objective of each project; the rationale for the placement and style of every element, color, or object; and how each part contributed to the overall effect and solution. That day I learned that not everybody thinks this way. That there is immeasurable value in the exploration, in the thinking, in the searching. Still today, there are countless designers who can blow me out of the water with their composition, knack for creating interesting color combinations, finesse with type, and Photoshop skills. But the reason my clients come back to me is because they value the *why* as much as the *what*.

I guess I've always wanted to know the *why*, and the questioning that served me well in design continued once I began to witness people who had an intimate, personal relationship with Jesus. My closest friends will attest to stories of intense conversations with me firing question after question at them. It's nothing short of a miracle that they stuck by me, allowing me to interrogate them and dispute things they believed to be facts. I asked anyone I thought might have an insight or answer, often forming the same question in multiple ways until I finally found an answer that satisfied me. I was as desperate to know and to understand as they were exhausted from trying to answer.

I've never stopped asking.

My friend Lisa offered what may be the single most valuable piece of advice I've ever received. After a grueling (for her) and enlightening (for me) four-hour drive home from a business trip in Chicago during which I relentlessly grilled her about God, the Holy Spirit, prayer, intercession, faith, ways people worship, and I can't remember what all else, she wrote me this note:

> My dear one,
>   You've started an important journey, and I am excited to see where it takes you. Now would be a good time to start a journal. Watch for "coincidences." If you keep your eyes open, you're likely to see God's fingerprints all over those coincidences. Write down what you see.

I can't imagine how different my spiritual life would be if I hadn't listened.

No matter how much we want to see and tell God's story, our time is spread thin. We're busy, emotional, weary, distracted, and fickle. Quick to demand answers and slow to remember. The things that matter so ridiculously much at this moment in time—well, the triumph or joy over one answer is eclipsed almost immediately by the next problem.

God's final answers are not necessarily the point. They're the equivalent of the completed design project, neatly mounted on a presentation board for everyone to see. I saved many of my college projects, but eventually the boards got bent and scuffed from being stuffed into the backs of closets, the colorful papers peeled off as the spray glue hardened, and they became victims of periodic office purges.

In my prayer journals, I have a chronicle of my relationship with God—an indisputable narrative of the divine insights, mundane happenings, powerful lessons, and overwhelming gratitude that filled those years.

But I still have the sketchbooks. And I have my prayer journals, which I treasure even more. In those pages, I have a record of my faith, a chronicle of my relationship with God—an indisputable narrative of the divine insights, bizarre coincidences, mundane happenings, powerful lessons, humbling revelations, and overwhelming gratitude that filled those years, that built my faith. That showed me God is real, and He loves me. My proof that God's Word is living and active and relevant.[25] The discoveries I made as I prayed—as I asked and begged and pleaded and yielded and wrestled and sought—gave me an accurate picture of the structure and nature of my heavenly Father. They forever changed the way I view myself, my loved ones, my church, my faith, and my God.

* * *

One night, I was skimming through my journal from July 2008, a month after Mom's cancer diagnosis. At that point, there was so much we didn't know. All we knew was that the statistics online were dismal, reporting that less than 4 percent of people with her specific diagnosis survive for one year. I wrote about a woman at church, Sandee, who—right in the middle of the choir song we were singing—pressed one hand into my back and the other on my stomach, and prayed. And prayed. I know Sandee well enough to know that she only acts when she feels a nudge from God, so I closed my eyes and tried not to worry about who saw us. Later, I wrote this:

> Sandee told me that God told her to touch my back—
> right there—and pray. She thinks it had to do with my
> mom. Mom goes in Tuesday for new scans and gets
> the results Thursday. Maybe God healed her—erased
> new growth or something. Maybe He took care of some
> immediate pain or problem. I don't know. But how sweet
> of Him to use Sandee—and allow me to be a part of
> it—since I seem to be having such a hard time praying
> right now.
>
> I write this down tonight in the hope that I will
> someday look back at this and know this was a time of
> healing. Complete, partial, I don't care. I just want to
> see evidence of God in here, in this. I want to find hope
> and moments of rejoicing. I want to find glory in the
> gracious, merciful healing powers of our Lord. I want
> my mom to be okay.

In 2009, I rejoiced in another journal about Mom's continued good health. She was taking a break from chemo; her hair was growing back. Now, more than two years after losing her, the words in both journals make me stumble. I'm just now finally getting past being mad at God for not healing her. But I also wonder—*did I maybe get it wrong? Did I remember it incorrectly?* According to my journal entries, it sounds like maybe He did.

It couldn't have been healing, I argue in my mind, *because Mom is dead.*

A quiet whisper pushes through: *She lived three years. They originally gave her months. That was healing.*

Maybe you're a skeptic. Maybe you're assuredly faithful. Or perhaps, like me, you're a faithful skeptic. But here's the thing I can't deny: The pages of my journals are saturated with an awareness of God and what He has done for me. I witnessed, experienced, and wrote it. When I read my words, written in my own hand, I can no longer fool myself into believing something else.

If you don't already keep a prayer journal, maybe it's time to start your own sketchbook. This is for your eyes only (and for His), and there is only one guideline: absolute truth. If you feel it, believe it, doubt it, hate it, or love it, write it. Don't hide what you really think, sugarcoat it, or try to make it pretty. This is not an art project that will be displayed for the world to see. You may hide it if you're worried about someone reading it. But this journal can become a valuable tool for you, a way to document your own personal process. To see God's active, involved presence, to discover what you believe and to explore how specific circumstances challenge or strengthen those beliefs. Because God isn't only found in the answers; He is found in truth and exploration. He becomes visible in the *process*.

> *A prayer journal can help you discover what you believe and explore how specific circumstances challenge or strengthen those beliefs. Because God isn't only found in the answers. He becomes visible in the process.*

That's because He *is* the process. The process by which it all makes sense. The process by which this sometimes painful, confusing, and contradictory life journey attains value.

When I don't know what to think or can't find words to pray, I sit down with my prayer journal. Sometimes I write *to* God, other times *about* God. Journaling keeps me focused since it engages my mind and my hand. Don't wait for an answer to get started. Remember, the value is in how you get to the answer. When I write, I don't have to give all the background—He knows—but I try to document the jumble of thoughts, questions and fears, emotions and events, what makes sense and what doesn't, because when I record those things along the way, I see change and growth over the long run. *Lord, You already know this, but here it is: I am confused, uncertain, conflicted, joyous, hopeful, troubled, or filled with despair. What am I supposed to understand about this? What do You want me to learn? What does Your Word teach me? How do I need to change? Am I wrong or right? Or does that even matter? Have I missed the point? Your Word says* this—*but how does that work in practice? Does it really mean what I thought it did?* And on and on.

I try to hold nothing back. I thank Him for my understanding of who He is and praise Him for loving me. I remember that He is able and worthy and that nothing is too hard for Him. I remember the other times I felt this way and how He carried me through other frightening, hopeless, frustrating, and sad situations. I remember the shape of God. I point my eyes toward the horizon. And there, in that place and against all logic, I find the truth (or at least *a* truth). When I finish, I may have clear direction about the next steps I need to take. I often know things I didn't know when I began. I may have seen the flaw in my own character that I need to work on, in spite of the qualities of the other person whose flaws I initially went to the Lord about.

These results have little to do with the problem prompting me to pray and everything to do with whom I'm praying to. Some might say I had the answers inside me already, and the process brought them out. Others would claim God spoke to me. Whatever it actually is, I personally believe He is behind the insights I find.

If blank pages intimidate you (as they do many), let me promise you that you are not required to perform, to use pretty words or neat handwriting, or to suddenly fabricate a book-worthy relationship with God. The empty pages are nothing more than hope. Possibility. A blank canvas. I believe that if I start writing, then I will see what I cannot already see. I believe that you will too.

But if you're hesitant to take that first step, fill the first page with your name. Include your contact information. Write your favorite Bible verse or a quote that inspires you. Write a dedication: *To the Maker of all that is seen and unseen.* Or *Okay, God, I'm here. Show me.* Or *I want to try this, but I feel incompetent. Help me.* Date it, doodle on it, anything to get past the first page so it is no longer a blank book. Take the first step to make it a conversation in process.

Like everything, it's all in how you choose to see it.

PRAYER PALETTE

If we begin with certainties, we will end in doubt. But if we begin with doubts and bear them patiently, we may end in certainty.
~FRANCIS BACON

WRITING PROMPTS. Not sure what to say when those blank journal pages are staring you in the face? Pick a prompt, set a timer if you want (start with ten minutes), and start writing. Don't stop to think. Don't let your pen stop moving until you are done. Just write.

In your heart, keep an attitude of offering, of openness. You can write about God, about your faith and beliefs, or—my preference—write *to* God. Talk to Him as though He is sitting there beside you.

WRITE A LOVE LETTER TO GOD:

- I love You because . . .
- My favorite thing about You is . . .
- I feel closest to You when . . .
- Today I saw You in [this person/situation] . . .

ASK HIM QUESTIONS OR BRING HIM YOUR DOUBTS:

- My biggest doubt is . . .
- What can I do for You?
- One thing that doesn't make sense to me is _____. Please help me understand.
- What's troubling me today is _____. Help me work through it.
- What stumbling blocks am I facing? How can I get past them?
- I disagree with this interpretation of Scripture. Show me the truth.
- I'm upset that You haven't answered my prayer.
- Why did you say _____?

REMIND YOURSELF OF ALL YOU KNOW ABOUT HIM:

- The aspect of You I am leaning on today is. . . [Provider, Counselor, Healer, Prince of Peace, the Good Shepherd, etc.]
- The first time I knew You were there was when . . .
- When I picture You, I see _____.
- A miracle I've witnessed is . . .

- I know You are real because . . .
- What surprises me the most about You is . . .
- You are so good. You are _____ [fill in names, titles, aspects, characteristics].
- I remember when You . . .

TELL GOD YOUR STORIES AND RETELL HIS:

- What You have revealed to me
- A specific time someone prayed for me
- How I hear Your voice
- What I believed about You in elementary school. As a teen. When my kids were born. When I lost a person close to me. When You first revealed Yourself to me.
- Lord, You've changed me. Over the last year, I've noticed . . .
- My earliest memory of You is . . .
- My favorite gift (or talent) You have given me (and what I'd like to do with it)
- I'll never forget the time You . . .
- Sometimes You feel far away from me when . . .

OR SIMPLY EXPLORE AND RECORD:

- The person who taught me most about prayer is . . .
- Ways to open my life to You
- Someone whose faith I admire is . . . (and why)
- What I would like my children to know about my faith is . . .
- A Scripture that means a lot to me is . . .
- I sometimes hide the fact that I am a Christian because . . .
- The thing I wish I could change about myself is . . .

- What I've learned from watching others (both good and bad)
- Thank You for giving me the strength to . . .
- A temptation I'm struggling with is . . .
- Forgive me, Lord, for . . .
- Thank You, Lord, for . . .
- I can't seem to forgive myself for . . .
- Help me to let go of my anger about . . .
- Teach me to forgive people who hurt me, like . . .

A person's relative importance is often depicted in artwork.

CHAPTER 14

TAKING THE
MEASURE OF THINGS

(PROPORTION)

Paint as you see and be accurate in your drawing:
the whole secret of your art is there.

WILLIAM BOUGUEREAU

Much of this book is about keeping your eyes open and trying to see what God is doing—not because we have a right to know, but because it's much easier to hang on through frustrating times when we can get a glimpse of what's to come. Faith, however, is blind. It's believing *in spite of* what you see. And being changed along the way. The reality is we may never know the end of a particular story. God may show Himself, or He may not. But even if we don't know, even if we don't see, it doesn't mean God isn't working, changing, effecting, delivering. It just means we happen to be unable to see it at the moment.

My friend Colleese has numerous health issues—multiple sclerosis, anaphylactic allergies, and seizures, among other things. One day, in the basement laundry room of her apartment building, sitting in her wheelchair, she felt an MS flare coming on. She was terrified. From experience, she knew that this wasn't going to be a brief wave of pain, but something that incapacitated her. She had no one to call, and she knew the risks inherent in it happening while she was alone. She wasn't falling prey to an overactive imagination. Her fears were well-founded.

Years before this night, she'd witnessed an event on TV in which people of many faiths came together during a choir rehearsal. They wanted to pray for a particular woman to be healed, but there was such diversity of religion that they decided, instead, to sing to her. One voice sang her name, and then another, then another. Sweet tenderness, swelling into a beautiful harmony. Colleese said you could see the change in the women in the group, holding hands, with tears on their faces as they prayed. They didn't have answers, so they lifted up their friend to the One who did. Her name—the song—was the prayer, and it bound them all together.

It also planted a seed in Colleese.

That night in the laundry room, she began to sing. As her strength melted from the pain, she had nothing left and needed

God. All she could do was offer herself, offer where she was and what she was experiencing, to God as her prayer. In that moment, it was literally all she had. No family, no one nearby to help. She knew her condition could be life-threatening, but she pushed out the fear that was crowding in. And she began to sing. Not a particular melody, just putting the words about her immediate situation into song. *I'm scared and I don't know what I'm going to do, how I'm going to survive down here for the next twenty minutes. I can't make my wheelchair go. . . .* She sang about where she was, and before long—even though the physical symptoms did not abate—the words evolved into something more and lifted her to a new place. *Thank You that I have enough clothes to have four washers full. Thank You that I live in a country where I don't have to wash by a river. Thank You for electricity. Thank You for money. Thank You for soap. Thank You that You have given me enough of a life that I have clothes that I was able to make dirty. Thank You.*

As she sang, the fear receded even though she was still in pain. She managed to get her clothes out of the washers and into dryers, fold them, and get both the laundry and herself upstairs to her apartment—singing the whole time. She told me, "I didn't physically change, but something changed inside because it was all real—spontaneous. Prayer-singing—no matter what I'm doing in life, if I sing *where I am*—this is my gift to Him. The only thing I can offer Him is 'here I am.'"

This isn't a story about a miracle cure, but in some ways it's even better. It's about a woman who offered all that she had—as little as it was—and found that it was enough. *He* is enough. For Colleese, and for you, and for me.

Before this, she often had trouble praying. She would over-think the words and be stuck, something many of us can relate to. When Colleese censored her prayers, they became not a holy thing but a head thing. That day in the basement, she learned that prayer, in the form of a personal song, is her sustenance. It comes from the depths of her soul. "Medically, I probably should not be alive today," she says. But she is. And not because she gets up at 5 a.m. to pray for half an hour a day, but because she never ceases. She offers all that she has, and she finds over and over again that it is enough. That God has carried her through. Sustained her. Changed her. And given her a valuable gift. She feels rich.

In the book of Mark, Mark recounts a moment when Jesus sat near the collection box at the entrance of the Temple, watching people bring their offerings. Later, He called together His disciples and told them about one woman's giving. "This poor widow has given more than all the others who are making contributions. For they gave a tiny part of their surplus, but she, poor as she is, has given everything she had to live on" (Mark 12:43-44). Jesus wasn't as moved by the wealthy people's contributions as He was with hers. It wasn't the value of the coins she gave, but the enormous cost of giving all that she had. He shows us that our measure of generosity and wealth, like so many other things, is upside down.

Colleese often had trouble praying. She would overthink the words and be stuck, something many of us can relate to. When Colleese censored her prayers, they became not a holy thing but a head thing.

Colleese inherently understands this. She knows that God needs nothing, and He deserves everything. She doesn't ask anything in return, just lifts up people and situations from her heart. She lets God decide where her prayers will go, for how long, and what tune she will sing. Even on the day when she was caught sitting in her wheelchair outside when a rainstorm hit. If that wasn't bad enough, an SUV sped through a puddle and drenched

Colleese and her service dog. Although she was in shock momentarily, Colleese found herself singing. *That's not very nice. Maybe they didn't know, maybe they didn't see me, but even if they did, I'm called to pray for them.*

It is the person who prays who is changed. The Bible confirms what Colleese discovered. "Confess your sins to each other and pray for each other so that you may be healed. The earnest prayer of a righteous person has great power and produces wonderful results" (James 5:16). "Pay attention to the language," she says. "It does not say 'so that the person you're praying for may be healed.' It says *you* (the one praying) may be. And that's one of the reasons we're called to pray."

She even prays in the pool, beginning and ending with laps of thanksgiving. "It's really a special place for me, being held up—and I'm not the one doing the holding. That's really a good picture of God." Her experience in the basement laundry room, and in the years since, has turned a formal relationship into a tender one. Colleese's prayer life went from forced and stilted to vibrant and real when she gave her physical being as her spiritual offering. When she offers herself—her body, her situation, her feelings—as prayer, every moment with Him is a gift.

And it all started because she took stock of where she was.

✷ ✷ ✷

Oftentimes, when an artist is drawing from life, she will extend her arm in front of her, pencil in hand, and use her thumb to mark off the length of an object. She will then compare that length to another—are these two objects the same width? Twice as long? One-third as wide? These measurements help her keep the objects in the drawing at the same relative size.

Colleese's prayer-singing is like the artist extending a pencil as a way of measuring the scale, angles, and positions of the objects she's drawing. In art, this technique is called "sighting," and it involves holding a pencil at arm's length, elbow locked, one eye closed. These positions must always be the same so that relative measurements are consistent. By measuring objects, the artist can reproduce the illusion of space accurately. When an object recedes in perspective, it gets shorter. The artist's mind might insist that the person in the background is as tall as the one in the foreground, but if one person is farther away, she can't draw him the same size on the paper without distorting the scene. Sighting is another way to override the knowledge stored in our brains that contradicts what our eyes actually see.

When Colleese sings to God, she's looking for an accurate representation of that moment. Not what she wants it to be, but what it *is*. That reality then becomes the basis of her offering, the foundation for her prayer. Like the artist, Colleese doesn't get to decide how things actually look, but she does her best to see clearly so that she has more to offer Him.

* * *

Ancient Egyptian artists used hieratic scale in their art—in other words, the size of an object denoted its relative importance. Kings and gods were several times larger than the common people. Sometimes you see this in the drawings of children. Mommy and Daddy are taller than the house because they dominate the child's world. Over many centuries, artists began to value accurate depiction of forms over hierarchical representation. In ancient Greek sculpture, you'll see the true proportions of the ideal human form. In the Renaissance, artists began to see the connection between proportion (size relationships) and the illusion of three dimensions—in other words, how the relative size of objects shows the distance of one element from another or from the viewer. Actually, size is only meaningful when it tells us about an object's dimensions in relationship to something else.

When you use proportion in prayer, first take stock of where you are and what you're dealing with. How big is this problem compared to the next? What *is* the problem? How close or far are you from God? Is God at the center of your composition (with regard to how you spend your money, time, and attention), or are you?

When you use proportion in prayer, first take stock of where you are and what you're dealing with. How big is this problem? How close or far are you from God?

Or simply, *This is where I am, Lord. I'm giving it to You.*

Whether you sing your prayers, write them, or speak them, whether they're long or short or detailed or abstract, proportion is a useful way to remember who God is. When Colleese began to sing in the basement that day, she knew she did not have anything else to offer. But she understood that *He* did. And she went to Him because she saw how big He is. How good. Not because He would do something for her, but just because of who He is. Because He is so much greater, and He deserved all that she had. *Everything* she had.

Colleese's song came from *praise*, not from *wanting*. Being with Him—as she was, as He is, without any demands or pleas—was all she wanted. *Everything* she wanted. As her song turned to praise, her attitude and understanding changed—a beautiful result from a pure intention.

In our culture, people go to great lengths to gain power, whether in politics or business, and even sometimes in churches. In our spiritual lives, we eventually come to accept that although there *is* power, *we* don't have it. When we acknowledge God's magnificence, goodness, and knowingness—His ability to see ahead of us and forgive what's behind us—then we've shifted the balance. We've traded in the illusion of our own power for the reality of His. We've recognized our need for Him and reinforced our understanding of our relative strengths. And once that's done, our only solution is to hand problems—any of them, all of them—over to Him. Trade what you have, sight unseen, for whatever He will give you. He has proven Himself more times than we can imagine. Not because He needed to prove how good He is, but because, as God, He can't help but be good.

Yet He wants to be involved. To hold us, oh so tightly, and sustain us. To change us in the middle of our darkest hours. And, in the process, to teach our hearts to sing.

PRAYER PALETTE

When the Spirit illuminates the heart, then a part of the man sees which never saw before; a part of him knows which never knew before, and that with a kind of knowing which the most acute thinker cannot imitate. He knows now in a deep and authoritative way, and what he knows needs no reasoned proof. His experience of knowing is above reason, immediate, perfectly convincing and inwardly satisfying. ~A. W. TOZER, THE DIVINE CONQUEST

Sometimes taking stock of our current situation can bring with it feelings of frustration, sadness, or anger. But it can also lead us toward gratitude, and focusing on feelings of thankfulness can help us let go of those ugly feelings.

WHEN OBLIGATION BECOMES OFFERING. I don't particularly enjoy doing housework, folding laundry, or cooking meals. It seemed unfair to me that simply because I am a woman, those tasks seemed to fall to me. But then I read something that changed the way I saw it. Instead of feeling burdened by the demands placed on me as a mom, I started thinking of it in a new way: I am taking care of my family, caring for the people God surrounded me with. When I take care of those people and things in my life, I'm being a good steward of His gifts. Therefore, when I do these things, if I dedicate each task to God, I can offer it up as prayer while I'm working. It becomes my offering, my sacrifice, my way of honoring the gifts He has given. And it changes the task profoundly.

As you go through your day, whether your tasks seem menial or profoundly important, keep up a running dialogue in your mind. *Lord, this is my offering to You. Thank You for the feet that wear these little socks. Thank You for the abundant food that dirtied these dishes. Clean my heart as I clean these plates. And accept this labor as an offering of thanksgiving.*

GRATITUDE JOURNAL. This isn't a new idea, but it's still a good one, with countless variations. When my girls were young, every night I wrote down three funny or sweet (or brilliant) things they said or did, whatever moments had sparked feelings of thankfulness. Later, the gratitude journal became a wonderful keepsake, bringing back those moments when Anna would try to bite Katie's toes in the bathtub, small steps of reconciliation in a friend's marriage, and the sweet simplicity of everyday moments as a family. You might start a list such as the one Ann Voskamp chronicled in her book *One Thousand Gifts: A Dare to Live Fully Right Where You Are*. At first, she was just trying to list a thousand grateful moments, but as she learned to notice each and every gift in the details of her day-to-day life, she didn't want to stop. Carry a notebook with you, and ask God to open your eyes to His beauty even in the darkest of moments.

Drawing the contours without peeking isn't easy to do, but it changes what you see.

CHAPTER 15

JUST KEEP GOING

(CONTOUR DRAWING)

*Contouring helps you see that the things you are drawing aren't
things but rather shapes that intertwine and connect.*

CHARLES REID, *PAINTING FLOWERS
IN WATERCOLOR WITH CHARLES REID*

A couple of years ago, I stepped outside into one of those breathtaking, beautiful winter mornings with fog everywhere—white snow melting into white sky, crisp frost tracing the curves of the branches. I was heading to Indianapolis to meet some friends, an hour's drive, so I grabbed my camera. The two-lane highway didn't have wide enough shoulders for me to safely pull over to capture the startlingly stunning scenes. Finally, after bypassing the perfect shot again and again because there was no place to stop, I vowed to take the next side road I came to. It snuck up on me in the fog, and I veered onto it, noticing moments too late that it was a rutted, muddy dirt road. Not even gravel, just dirt. *Great. My clean white car . . .*

I hadn't gone far before I regretted my decision, but there was no place to stop and nowhere to turn around. There was not a single house or lane to be found. At first the road was just messy and bumpy, but before long I started composing in my head the words I'd use to explain to my husband how I managed to become stranded in the middle of nowhere and in need of my knight in shining armor to rescue me. The thick muck sucked at my tires. My car was sliding from side to side when it wasn't bogged down by the wet earth trying to pull it under, and the tires were spinning, spewing mud up to the top of the side windows. At that point, I didn't care how clean my car was. All I could do was pray out loud and focus on *not stopping.* I knew if I so much as slowed down I'd never get moving again.

The sludge in the road pulled the car from left to right and back and forth. My shoulders were tense from gripping the wheel, and I repeated over and over, out loud, "Lord Jesus, please. Lord Jesus, please. Lord Jesus, PLEASE!" I couldn't form any prayers more eloquent, any thoughts more coherent. I just wanted out of there and couldn't stop to think about it or I'd never make it.

After two miles, I came to a crossroads (*Thank You, Jesus*) with a paved road (*Thank You, Jesus!*). With a deep breath of relief and a prayer that no one else was approaching the intersection, because I certainly couldn't stop and look, I turned onto it. Now that I was out of danger I felt foolish and annoyed. I headed directly back to the highway, making sure at each turn that the road was solid asphalt before me, and stopped at the first car wash I passed. I got out to make sure I hadn't exaggerated the whole thing. I hadn't. Mud was splattered all the way to the roof. Over lunch, I told my friends the story, a story that still makes them laugh until they cry.

I understand their amusement, but that's not what resonates with me. What does is praying when "just keep going" is all we can think, do, or feel. The idea has a parallel in drawing: blind contour drawing, which is drawing the outline of the subject without ever looking down at your paper or lifting your pencil. You choose a point along the edge of the subject and place the point of your pencil on the page, and then, going very slowly, move the pencil in coordination with your eye movements as you trace the shape. You don't lift your pencil or look down at the drawing until it is complete.

Drawing this way is hard. But it is another method, like drawing upside down, that releases your mind from defining and therefore prejudging a shape. Blind contour drawing helps teach you to identify the underlying structure and the overall mass of the object in its three dimensions. It can show you how different forms are related, that the top of one shape may be the bottom of another, and so on. And it teaches you to rely on instinct.

The trick to drawing this way is to keep your eyes on the subject at all times. Stop thinking, and just *look*.

When we're praying, we need to keep our eyes on Jesus. I take that back—not *just* when we're praying. When we're working. Eating. Playing. Helping. Doubting. Loving. Hurting. Parenting. Spending. Dreaming. Living.

We may be in unwanted situations that are a result of our own choices (or rash decisions). We have control less often than we'd like. If you do have it, and you're aware that the road you're following isn't the right one—either because it goes to the wrong place or because dangers lurk alongside it—well, then, by all means, get off that path as soon as you possibly can.

When we're praying, we need to keep our eyes on Jesus. I take that back—not just when we're praying. When we're working. Eating. Helping. Doubting. Loving. Hurting. Dreaming. Living.

If only it were always that easy.

But so much is beyond our control. A relative is diagnosed with AIDS or cancer or Alzheimer's. We lose jobs or friends or money. We're misunderstood or unappreciated or wronged. Our kids fail, rebel, or turn away. Our spouses lose their passion and look elsewhere. Our bodies fall apart. Temptation rears its ugly head. Whether large or small, these predicaments can feel, if not actually *be*, life-altering and all-consuming. You might think you can't bear it. Your heart is broken, your strength is gone, your patience is depleted. And you are tired, oh so weary. It's too heavy, too much, and you don't know how to keep going. It's like you're being pulled down into the quagmire, under the sludge and muck, trapped and unable to find a way back to dry ground.

It might be easier just to stop.

Time and time again, King David found himself in a pit, but he never hesitated to cry out for help.

I waited patiently for the LORD;
    he turned to me and heard my cry.
He lifted me out of the slimy pit,
    out of the mud and mire;

he set my feet on a rock
   and gave me a firm place to stand.
PSALM 40:1-2, NIV

The value of contour drawing is that it helps us determine the form of an object. Praying this way involves keeping our eyes on Him. Looking to God for direction, for help, for strength and comfort and companionship—these things reveal the shape of the God we serve. The shape of the divine undergirding the terrain we're traveling. Leading us through just as soon as we relinquish control.

The keyword is *through*. Throughout the Bible, God leads people through some major things: *through* the Red Sea onto dry ground,[26] *through* the valley of the shadow of death.[27] In Isaiah 43:2, God tells Jacob,

When you go through deep waters,
   I will be with you.
When you go through rivers of difficulty,
   you will not drown.
When you walk through the fire of oppression,
   you will not be burned up.

The sooner we take our eyes off the doubt, fear, worry, or pain and look instead at Him, the sooner we will see Him. And the more we see of Him, the more we can trust Him. Believe that He knows the right way out. He may not take the most direct route. It might be a longer road than we imagined, with rescue a long way off. There might be potholes and detours, and we may lose our bearings. But we *will* emerge eventually—even if we are just a little bit muddy (or maybe a lot).

When you feel you are running for your life—fleeing trauma

or fear or grief or abandonment or failure—prayer becomes more critical than ever. The more extreme the situation, the more trouble we have forming words into coherent prayer. Usually there's no time to contemplate or evaluate or even decide if we *want* to pray. We just do because we have to. In these moments, I'd like to suggest something radical: *Don't think about it.* Let loose from your gut. Passionately, emotionally. Don't worry about the words. Romans 8:26 (NIV) says that the Holy Spirit helps us when we don't know what to pray by interceding, not with words, but through "wordless groans."

When you are making a blind contour drawing, the finished drawing is usually a simple, outlined view; although, it often shows a surprising level of detail. You can complete your drawing quickly and accurately by following your gut (and your eyes, of course).

In your spiritual life, you will have seasons of flowery, eloquent prayers; times for seeking out subtleties and nuances; and moments of determining your life purpose and spiritual gifts. But some seasons are desperate, primary, fundamental. They run deeper than your intellect or reason. At these times, don't hesitate to say it like it is, to be blunt, to cut straight to the heart of the matter. *Help me. Fix it. Heal her. Be with them. Speak to him. Save us.* Or, even more simply, the only words I could think as I slogged through the mud: *Please, Lord Jesus. Please.*

Even if you're in a sunshiny place spiritually, your words may not reflect that. Have you ever been overwhelmed to the point of being speechless with gratitude? Tucking the blanket around your baby, resting your hand on his chest to feel his breaths. Making eye contact with your spouse to share a private joke, a jolt of connection in the midst of a roomful of people. Opening the official envelope to see the word "Congratulations!" Seeing a friend turn to God for the first time. Managing not to bounce those three checks last night. Large or small, whatever it is, I am convinced

God loves it when we respond from deep within, bypassing reason and logic and just uttering the most heartfelt, profound truths. *Thank You. You are amazing. I love You. You are so good.*

We will not always get what we want, but when we learn to respond to each little gift along the way, it helps us cope when we're faced with disappointment. It reminds us that there may be a big no, but there have been many smaller yeses. Whether a season is abundant or lacking, whether the desired result didn't happen soon enough or lasted way too long, you will eventually emerge from one season into another. You'll make it to a paved road, drive through the car wash, your friends will get tired of you telling the story, and it will be over.

Except for one difference: you. You've conquered the fear, resisted the temptation, looked in the face of your biggest nightmare. God carried you through, and now you *know.* You no longer have to wonder if you can survive the unthinkable, recover from the most devastating of blows. True, the answers to your prayers may be hard to understand. But the One who answers them remains faithful, constant, eternally and perpetually good and merciful and just—even when the answer hurts or seems unfair or makes no earthly sense. He is the horizon that never moves, that goes on forever, farther than you can see.

> *Faith means trusting that He will do what's right, and believing that even if the outcome is not what we want, being in it with God is better than being anywhere else without Him.*

We may not know *how* He will answer, what steps He will take, or the methods He will use to resolve the situation. We don't necessarily always get to witness a resolution or an end to the problem. If we look closely enough, though, as we travel through, we might see the form below the surface. This can happen only if we keep our eyes focused on God. We don't get to choose the answer we want. We don't get to decide if it's the *right* answer (in our minds) or when (or *if*) He will reveal it to us. But we do get to make a choice: faith or fear.

Faith means trusting that He will do what's right, and believing that even if the outcome is not what we want, being in it *with* God is better than being anywhere else *without* Him. Authors and moviemakers have long envisioned the future. Jumping forward and back in time, scripting how it all ends up. Changing something that sets a string of events into motion. We want to find a way to feel in control because of all the unknowns. Will the tumor come back? Will cutting red meat out of my diet lower my blood pressure enough? How far can my son push the boundaries before he gets expelled? Will they drop the lawsuit or won't they? Even people of strong faith sometimes walk through their days on pins and needles, dwelling on all the unknowns.

But if you think about it, the biggest, most critical factor is not unknown. Every story we read of the Lord's life—every act He accomplished and parable He told, the experience and ramifications of His crucifixion and His resurrection—reveals who He is, shows Him to us, and proves that we can count on Him. So though you might be scared of a particular thing—a test, an interview, a breakup, a loss—you don't need to be scared of the God who will take you through it. You just need to look for Him. Look *at* Him.

Just like the artist who uses contour drawing to train his hand to go where his eye does, we can apply this concept spiritually to teach ourselves to behave like the One we're watching. To follow His actions, repeat His words, build on the foundation of stability that He provides. To love and care and help as He would.

The reality is, no matter how pure my intentions and genuine my faith, I won't be able to live it like He did. Or the same way you do. And you won't do it like the next person. Using the principles of contour drawing, our drawings may never be perfect, but they will improve with practice. Aspiring to live like God is not easy or peaceful. Don't think there won't be bumps in the road. Because, like any adventure, sometimes it can be a wild ride.

But I promise you, He's there with you. Steering the vehicle. Calming the storm. And pointing the way through the quagmire.

PRAYER PALETTE

Faith . . . is the art of holding onto things . . . in spite of your changing moods. ~C. S. LEWIS, MERE CHRISTIANITY

PERSONALIZE IT. Find a verse in the Bible that resonates with you, that seems to speak to a specific situation or need. Then pray through it, substituting someone else's name (or your own) for a pronoun or other name. Psalm 91:1-4 might become:

> *Those who live in the shelter of the Most High*
>> *will find rest in the shadow of the Almighty.*
> *This I declare about the Lord:*
> *He alone is **Rick's** refuge, **Rick's** place of safety;*
>> *he is **Rick's** God, and **Rick** [will] trust him.*
> *For he will rescue **Rick** from every trap*
>> *and protect **Rick** from deadly disease.*
> *He will cover **Rick** with his feathers.*
> *He will shelter **Rick** with his wings.*
> *His faithful promises are **Rick's** armor and protection.*

HAND IT OVER. When you're in the middle of something big, your prayer life might go to one extreme or the other—either you find yourself in constant prayer, or you shut down and can't pray at all. When you can't seem to pray, be assured of two things: God knows your heart and can work anyway, and your friends probably feel helpless and would love to help carry you through this time by praying for you. All you have to do is ask—and then rest in the comfort of knowing your prayers aren't being neglected.

A friend of mine told me about a time when she was insanely attracted to a man she knew through work. They had an easy, instant rapport, and the attraction was apparent to everyone around them. She knew it was bad news—he was a great guy, but she absolutely did not want to mess up her marriage (or his). And she couldn't avoid him because of work. She knew she should pray, but she just couldn't muster up any conviction. She couldn't ask God to take this man out of her life because she knew, deep down, she didn't want him to go away. She was soaking up the attention. Yet she knew it would not end well without some intervention. So she asked a close friend to commit to praying for her—because the friend could, without feeling conflicted, pray for her marriage to be strengthened, for the attraction to go away, for God to intervene and put some distance between them. If you're in a situation in which you don't feel able to pray with sincerity—if you feel yourself in any kind of danger whatsoever—hand your prayers over to someone you trust to carry them for you until you can do it yourself.

Sometimes the best artwork is made on a nontraditional canvas.

CHAPTER 16

"WHERE DID I PUT MY SHOE?"

(OR WHAT ARE YOU WAITING FOR?)

I don't want to get to the end of my life and find that I lived just the length of it. I want to have lived the width of it as well.

DIANE ACKERMAN

Several years ago, my friends Peggy, Glenna, Tami, and I were feeling old and boring and restless, trapped in middle America with no water to be seen in any direction. I'm blaming it on geography, on miles and miles of flat fields, but maybe it was a midlife crisis. Either way, we needed a convertible. The only thing standing in our way? Money. What else is new? Inspired by a crazy flamingo car someone else drove around town—an old black convertible with pink flamingos glued on all sides and a giant bandage over a crumpled fender—we gave my husband an unusual task. One day he went to an auto auction and then pulled into our driveway with a faded white, past-her-prime 1989 Oldsmobile Ninety-Eight on a flatbed trailer. Not long after, with the help of a Sawzall, a dead-blow hammer, and Tim's muscle power, we had a convertible. Maybe *convertible* is the wrong word, since it didn't actually *convert*. It was simply a car with no top and a giant pink swimming noodle glued around the sharp, rough metal edge of the windshield. But in Indiana, in the throes of the emotional trauma brought on by nearing age forty, it was close enough.

His part done, Tim handed over the car. One of my habits is doing things to excess, so I was perfectly suited to the task before me. As a graphic designer and the designated art director for this project, I began with a roll of blue masking tape and beige fleckstone spray paint, transforming the lower sides of the car into a grainy, sandy beach. After covering the new "beach" with old newspapers, Peggy and I transformed the remaining grimy white metal into a shimmery sky with mottled, metallic blue spray paint.

I spent an afternoon with my paint brushes adorning the hood with a swirly, spirally sun in vibrant yellows and oranges, then added palm trees on each side. Peggy and Tami hot-glued fake flowers around the rearview mirror and pink faux fur to the dash. We strung garlands of blue silk hyacinths around the windshield and backseat, intertwining strands of plastic bananas and pineapples. We dangled silk leis and sandal air fresheners from the mirror, covered the floor with fuzzy pink bath mats, and turned striped beach towels into colorful seat covers. We worked into the night, laughing, singing, and laughing some more. The foofaraw included a fake grass skirt undulating from the rear bumper and a beach umbrella sticking up proudly—if wobbly—from the center of the parked car.

She definitely had a forceful personality, but she needed a name. More than just a car, she was a gaudy woman with over-the-top style. Her name should be equally exotic—a little sexy, a little daring, and a lot of fun. We named her Lola and played her song, "Copacabana," loudly from a portable CD player in the driveway. "She was a showgirl, with yellow feathers in her hair . . ." Thank you, Barry Manilow.

In spite of the simple joy we found in the work, real life beckoned. I'm sure that's happened to you, too—work deadlines loomed, the kids had games and practices, the weather wasn't nice enough (or was so nice we didn't want to be stuck in the garage), and Lola sat there, abandoned and awaiting the final touches, possibly muttering in her pistons about what fickle friends we were. *I'm good enough when no one else is around, but as soon as they get busy, I'm tossed aside.*

But when a man from church decided to host a car show in memory of his brother and asked us to bring our showgirl, Lola was suddenly in the forefront of our minds again. Two days before the show, the four of us were inspired to finish Lola's makeover.

Honestly, inspiration didn't have much to do with it at all. In fact, leaving home to go paint was the last thing I wanted to do. Not that I was all that excited about being home, either. That day, I'd left all three grumpy kids at home under the unenthusiastic care of my twelve-year-old. They took turns calling, crying, and arguing: "Do we really have to watch *That's So Raven*?" and "It's not fair because Anna ate the last soft pretzel."

Can anyone else relate?

Because it was raining, Lola was parked inside Tami's tiny one-car garage, leaving barely enough room for us to squeeze past each other. The garage door was open to let in some light. Contorting my body to remain protected from the elements, I tried to letter a flamboyant "Lola" signature onto the back of the car. I was cramped, uncomfortable, and tired of the whole thing. The Rollerball paint pen wouldn't give me an even flow of paint, and the brush was too soft. I couldn't get a strong, hard edge, couldn't find the right angle, and had nothing to rest my hand on. My kids kept calling my cell phone with one whiny complaint after another. I'm a perfectionist, my back hurt, and there was a mud puddle on the driveway right behind the corner of the car where I was.

Cue the ominous background music.

Already at the end of my patience, my foot slipped in the middle of that puddle and slid through the mud, pulling something in my back and activating my redheaded Irish anger. I let loose a word that will not be printed and then kicked my foot to dislodge the sticky mud. One of the backless tennis shoes I was wearing sailed up onto the long, low roof of the neighbor's house (and I thought I wasn't athletic). I stomped around in circles, cussing and crying, the one remaining shoe clomping against the cement while my soggy, muddy sock quietly thudded in response.

Peggy walked over to me, put her hand on my shoulder, and said, "Honey, go home. It's not worth it. This is supposed to be fun." She was right. I drove home with one bare foot, alternating between anger and embarrassment.

* * *

The next day was much better. I wore two shoes and kept them both on. Tami's son, Stephen, baked chocolate chip cookies for us. We accessorized with contributions from other friends. (QVC, you have nothing on us.) Lola was adorned with a sunny antenna ball from which flowed a spiral windsock. The fuzzy pink dashboard boasted a magnetic clipboard that exclaimed "Aloha" when you pressed the button, and on Lola's hood was the *pièce de rèsistance*, a ten-inch high carved coconut monkey our friend Marcia brought from Hawaii just for this purpose. Tami and Peggy spray painted Lola's wheels hot pink. Glenna hot-glued a palm tree and hundreds of shells (from Tami's recent trip to Florida) along the top of the backseat along with a giant rubber pineapple. We decorated the trunk with a silk parrot and a small boogie board found at a yard sale. Then we high-fived and admired our outrageous handiwork.

Secretly, I was terrified someone would see me driving her.

Labor Day dawned, and it was time to deliver Lola. I had been worrying about how people at the car show would react. These people were serious restorers and collectors—and, well, we were not. The other girls were busy, so Peggy drove Lola, and I followed in my car, safely out of the limelight.

The car show was held at a small city park. Balloons bounced in the wind. A local man, Tom, was there—as he was at all local festivals—selling his famous barbecue sandwiches and twisty potato chips out of a truck. Our youth pastor, Scott, was set up in a small striped tent, hunkering in the shade as he played oldies on loud, static-filled speakers. Lola preened among the vintage, gleaming, airbrushed machines. I was as embarrassed for her as if her dress had been tucked into the back of her panty hose. Parked jauntily in a corner, with her colorful back end facing the crowd, Lola was surrounded by giggling kids. The owners of the "real" cars stayed in their lawn chairs shaded by sun umbrellas, mumbling to their wives, waiting awhile before casually (and disdainfully) strolling close enough to get a better look.

Peggy and I stood back and watched Lola's paparazzi for a moment before I had to go home and work. Peggy stayed behind with Lola, and later that afternoon, she called. At first, I couldn't hear her words over the revelry and shouting around her. Then I figured out what she was saying. "Lola has just been named Best of Show!" Our colorful girl received the popular vote. We got the biggest, gaudiest trophy of all—fitting for the occasion. A few minutes later, I heard a horn honking outside the house. I ran out front to see Lola basking in all her kitschy glory. Peggy's kids hoisted the shiny trophy in triumph from the backseat. I hopped in and we drove around town, rejoicing with the kind of exhilaration one feels for an unlikely champion.

Although this adventure took place a few years ago, the memory lives on. Recently, Nathan referred to the day I lost my shoe. "That was the best day of my life!" Peggy exclaimed, clapping. I think she was exaggerating a teensy-weensy bit. It's hard for me to laugh at my less-than-shining moment. But it's still a good story, and it illustrates something important about creating.

Sometimes it's fun and everything goes smoothly. But that's usually when we *want* to do it. When conditions are ideal, nobody is pressuring us, and we have exactly the right tools and a clearly defined plan. Sometimes, however, we have to perform under pressure because there is a deadline we've put off, which can make us grouchy, tense, and distracted. We can approach it gracefully, or we can kick our shoes onto the roof. Which feels really good in the moment, but right after the satisfying release comes regret and shame. I was mortified that Tami's husband, Lane, had to ask his neighbor that night if he could climb onto his roof and retrieve the object of my grown-up temper tantrum. It's not pretty when your friends see your ugly side, which is why I heeded Peggy's suggestion to call it a day.

In the end, after sitting for weeks waiting to be finished, Lola made her perfectly acceptable debut to the delight of the children and other showgoers. How her story unfolded is uncomfortably close to a prayer pattern I sometimes find myself in.

Just like my friends and I put off finishing Lola, I often put off prayer. There's not a deadline, right? I mean, God is always there. And He'll always listen. I'll wait until it's convenient, until the conditions are just right. Until I feel like it. I'll do it after I get dinner in the Crock-Pot because *that has to happen right now.* Oh, and I'll pray *after* I call about the extra charges on my cell phone bill. But before I know it, I've paid the other bills too. Filed some papers. Straightened my desk. Whipped up a pan of brownies for the bake sale. Talked to three clients on the phone, deposited the check that came in the mail in the bank, stopped for a cup of coffee to take home, and talked for half an hour to a friend who was at the coffee shop, before remembering a hair appointment I have in five minutes.

> *I often put off prayer. There's not a deadline, right? I mean, God is always there. And He'll always listen. I'll wait until it's convenient. Until I feel like it.*

Sure, it's nice to be productive. But not when I'm filling my life with busyness and neglecting the truly important activity of prayer. It's not about God needing to hear from *me* that minute. It's about the fact that *I* need *Him.* I fill my time—as we all do—with the things that are important to me. And if I'm not intentional, if I don't stop right now to pray, then time slips by and I miss the opportunity. Before I know it, the kids are home. Backpacks are unloaded, homework is due, stomachs are growling, and another day has passed without Him. I've missed out, and it's all because I was waiting for the ideal moment. For the living room to be picked up and the house to be quiet and for me to be in the mood and for having just the right words or the right journal with smooth, white paper and faint narrow lines and a pen that doesn't glob and the perfect worship song playing on the stereo.

When I surprise myself with the sheer number of trivial items I'm marking off my to-do list, I usually find it's because I'm avoiding the important things. I'm probably not feeling distinctly unspiritual—I'm probably just tired. Lazy. It's because life feels out of control and I'm attempting to impose some control. It could be because I've prayed about the same things without seeing results for too long. Or because I'm overwhelmed by the number of huge, tragic situations in desperate need of divine intervention. Or because I've stayed away from God for so long that I'm embarrassed to come back now. I'm ashamed to ask Him to retrieve my shoe, so I just don't go to Him at all.

Whatever the specifics, it all boils down to one thing: I'm not feeling inspired. When I refuse to pray, it's a temper tantrum, just less dramatic. I'm being a diva, wanting circumstances to line up just right. If I would sit down and start, it might not be the most enlightening spiritual moment of my life. But maybe it would be. Maybe that's the precise moment when God will choose to turn my world around. If it's not, however, it doesn't mean the prayer time is any less valuable. Prayer gets its value from the One we're praying to, not from the one doing the praying.

My dad modeled what dedication to his art meant. Every morning, when he wasn't golfing, I watched my dad walk out to his studio right after breakfast to work. He painted nearly every day, whether the paintings were selling well or not, whether he had a show coming up soon or nothing planned, whether he was feeling energetic or sad or lackadaisical. I don't remember ever hearing him say, "I don't feel inspired so I can't paint today." There were days when the end result wasn't good. Sometimes he would start with a 30″ x 40″ piece of watercolor board, and by the time he cropped out the problem areas, he'd be left with an 11″ x 14″

image. But the next day, he rose from the breakfast table, went right back to the studio, and tried again.

He did this every weekday, over and over and over again. The outcome of his dedication, his consistent practice? He is good. Very good. He supported our family from the time I was a year old, solely by selling his art. He won awards and received recognition, but he's not featured in art history books or in New York art galleries. What is most impressive to me is that he embraced the joy that comes from using the abilities God gave him, and he has continued to be grateful for the opportunity to do what he loves. Now, at seventy-six, he's semiretired, but when he talks about his work, his enthusiasm still shows: "I *got* to paint today."

Through discipline and focus, Dad honed his skills and learned that he could create in all kinds of situations and circumstances. We can too. One of the most amazing gifts God gives us is *access*. We are *allowed* to come to Him. Not only that, He *wants* us to. Every day, no matter how crowded our calendars are.

Prayer doesn't require specific abilities or unbearably hard work. It just requires showing up. Participating. Repeating. It's not supposed to be drudgery, and if you find it to be, it's time to shake things up a little. Try something new. Some days may not be as exciting as others, but every single bit of effort is valuable. Dad's paintings are not always perfect, but over the past fifty years, he has created a significant body of work, a reputable career in art. A life of joy.

In prayer, our focus isn't on reputations but on *relationship*. No effort will ever be thrown out for not being good enough. In fact, I don't recall seeing a single instance in the Bible when someone was told his or her prayers weren't good enough—except when the prayers were merely for show, inauthentic because they did not come from the heart. Since the power of prayer is dependent on the One who has all power, not on our own abilities, you will be a part of something great just by showing up.

The day of the unfortunate shoe incident, I painted even though I didn't want to, and I'm not proud of how I behaved. But now I look back and see that that one less-than-perfect day was part of something bigger and better. I am one-fourth owner of a big, shiny, gaudy Best of Show trophy. After we'd displayed the trophy in the church fellowship hall for a while, my friends let me bring it home. Now, whenever someone brings up this story, our feelings are bittersweet. I'm sad to report that Lola's transmission failed, she subsequently got waterlogged sitting in a parking lot, and eventually we had to tow her to the dump. Still, though, the memories make my friends and me laugh. And although I threw a heinous grown-up hissy fit that put my kids' tantrums to shame, my relationships with my friends grew deeper. They loved me through the mess and forgave me. So many good things happened because of Lola.

Since the power of prayer is dependent on the One who has all power, not on our own abilities, you will be a part of something great just by showing up.

When it comes to prayer—or any tasks God gives you—don't wait for just the right moment. This is it. Dive in right now. And trust that God will bring value to your efforts to create, whether you are decorating with hot pink spray paint and plastic pineapples or not.

PRAYER PALETTE

You cannot become a master until you actually take the leap, do the work, make several thousand mistakes, and live to tell about it.
~*SUZANNE FALTER-BARNS*

Jump right in. Try these approaches that keep your hands busy and use objects you may have at home—and begin praying right now.

PRAYER STRING. Grab a hole punch and a piece of string at least a yard long. (If you don't have string, use ribbon from your gift-wrapping supplies or the drawstring that fell out of your favorite hoodie.) Cut a few sheets of paper or index cards into strips (around 4" long and wide enough to write on), then punch a hole near one end. Write your prayer requests (for yourself and for others) onto the strips of paper. Thread the string through the hole and tie a knot. A few inches down the string, add another, and then another.

Pause at each knot to pray. As prayers are answered, you can pull off the strips of paper. Adapt this for a prayer group by having each person tie his or her personal requests onto a separate piece of string and then trade with each other, praying for the other person's needs through the week, one knot at a time.

PRAYER STONES. Collect smooth stones on your next walk by the creek, or buy a bagful at a craft store. Using a permanent marker or paint, write key words on each—*finances, client relationships, our pastors, a couple struggling with infertility, a friend's daughter's health, names of friends and family.* Keep them in a bowl or tray. Hold each in your hand as you pray, or pick one up every time you walk by. You can do something similar by writing prompts on Popsicle sticks and keeping them in a mug on your desk. Or consider writing on slips of colored paper and placing them in a glass jar.

PINTEREST PRAYERS. Start a private board and pin pictures of your family and friends, people from Facebook, celebrities and national figures, articles and news stories about world events, and the like. When you pray, click through your board and pray for the people you have included. You can also do this on paper. Put pictures in a notebook or photo album, then pray through the pages. Or hang the photos on a bulletin board. Write your thoughts over or around the images if you have any insights as you pray. Another idea is to grab a newspaper and thick marker, and pray about the specific situations and people represented on the pages (writing things like "bring unity," "erase those images from her mind," etc.).

Magnifying a printed piece reveals what it is made of.

CHAPTER 17

SEEING PAST
THE DOTS

(POINTILLISM)

*Creativity is not the finding of a thing, but the
making something out of it after it is found.*

JAMES RUSSELL LOWELL

Just as sometimes it helps to break a large picture into smaller sections (the grid method), at other times an artist intentionally creates innumerable small pieces that together form a larger, comprehensive picture. One of these styles is pointillism, a technique developed in the late 1800s by Georges Seurat and Paul Signac, in which the artist creates an image out of distinct dots of pure color, relying on the ability of the viewer's eyes and mind to blend the color spots into a full range of tones. Up close, it may be hard to tell what the image is, but when you step back you can see the whole picture.

My high school precalculus teacher understood this concept. Early in my senior year, the girl who had been my best friend since elementary school turned on me. Most of our class had been invited to a party being given by a girl we ate lunch with every day—but not me. I covered two sheets of notebook paper with a letter to my friend about how I didn't understand why nobody liked me, and I'd never felt like I fit in because I liked different music, clothes, etc. She then proceeded to prove to me just how much I didn't belong, as I walked around the corner and saw the rest of my lunch group reading—and laughing at—the letter meant for my friend's eyes only.

We'd chosen seats beside each other in all of our classes, so she was able to ignore me from a close distance until the day we sat side by side in the gym, as valedictorian and salutatorian, trying not to bump elbows at graduation. In the meantime, tired of walking the halls on my own before school, sick of pretending I liked being by myself, I made friends with some other girls. Caving to peer pressure, I let one of them copy answers over my shoulder on a big math test. I thought we had gotten away with it until my perfect paper came back the next day with a big red zero on it.

When Mr. Hopkins asked me to stay after class, I couldn't look him in the eye as I braced for a lecture. I'd always loved his class and, truth be told, I had a bit of a crush on him. We sat down, and he didn't speak for a moment. I finally looked up and he sighed. "Just hang in there 'til college, Kelly. If you can just get through high school, you are really going to be great. You'll really do something. Just hold on."

He got it. He saw way past the issue at hand, still giving me consequences (a zero on the test, which brought me down to an unheard-of C for the grading period)—but because he saw that there was a bigger picture, he didn't need to dwell on one specific dot or berate me for what I did wrong. He knew I knew. And he apparently understood my reasons but didn't discuss that. Instead, he showed me that there was a bigger picture and begged me to hold on until I could see it too. Until I could understand that, as bad as that moment might be, it was just one teeny tiny dot and not the complete picture.

I'm not the only one who's ever felt rejected, betrayed, or alone. It's comforting to know that Jesus held out His hand to those who were shunned, including a man with leprosy. "When the man saw Jesus, he bowed with his face to the ground, begging to be healed. 'Lord,' he said, 'if you are willing, you can heal me and make me clean.' Jesus reached out and touched him. 'I am willing,' he said. 'Be healed!' And instantly the leprosy disappeared" (Luke 5:12-13).

I know you've probably ridden the roller-coaster ride of acceptance too. In elementary school, I was tall, smart, and klutzy, with red hair and freckles. (Truthfully, I've never outgrown that.) Playground chants of "I'd rather be dead than red on the head" don't begin to compare with the way lepers were shunned, or the way I was ignored my senior year, or some of the very real discrimination, bigotry, and bullying you might have experienced—but to an eight-year-old, it was a big deal. For years, I hunched over, pretended not to know all the answers, and tried to accept my poor genetic luck. Until tenth grade, when one of the popular girls dyed her hair red. I may not have fit in any better, but I felt better for a short time.

Our society's standards are subjective and fluid. We can't keep up, people won't always like us—the fact is, sometimes we just don't fit in. That doesn't consume me anymore because Jesus accepts me just as much as He does you. He won't hold any of us at arm's length. He won't be looking behind us, hoping someone better will come along. He'll reach out, touch us, and make us into the person He thinks we should be. The person who fits exactly in the spot He created us to fill.

"Seeking God's will" is a popular phrase heard in church circles. It sounds lofty, nebulous, ethereal, far-off—not like something we might actually attain. In all honesty, we may never have a clear picture of what it means. If we knew the details of all that will happen in our lives, pride might consume us, or we might huddle up in the corner underneath a blanket, afraid to step foot outside. But we needn't be afraid. Take that dot in pointillism. Up close, it doesn't look like much. But stand back, and it plays an important part in the composition. That's all that God's will is. The part He wants each of us to play. The individual dot He assigns to each of us.

If we knew the details of all that will happen in our lives, pride might consume us, or we might huddle up in the corner underneath a blanket, afraid to step foot outside.

Ancient tapestries in museums often depict stunning, elaborate scenes. And while some very fine weavings such as Turkish prayer rugs are equally impressive on the front and the back, some of the most beautiful tapestries look chaotic from behind, with ratty, tangled, and knotted threads. I like to think that when God watches over the world, He's looking at this gorgeous tapestry of all that He knows. Of all that we—individually and collectively—can be. We see the tangled knots, the individual messes that don't look all that great from this angle, but God's view of the beauty is never obscured.

If we're fortunate, sometimes God will give us a glimpse of that scene, just as He did when I was trying to sell my house (chapter 1). When He demonstrated that the result I'd sought was more effective and farther-reaching on His terms and through His timing, I had the strength to hold on. The individual dots—not being able to pay my bills, wanting to sell the house—took my attention away from the scene He was painting. The one in which I learned to trust Him for my provision. The one in which I endured financial hardship for a limited time in order for God to help Rosanne prepare for the long term.

If you want to see what picture God is painting for you, you have to stop focusing on that single dot. Don't get bogged down by the details when you pray. Look at the forest, not the individual trees. Take in the painting of a picnic by the sea instead of a single dot of paint. The gorgeous tapestry, not one tangled knot. I can't say it enough: We don't always get to know the reasons behind the way life's situations play out, and we won't always be witness to the final result. But if we watch, if we pray, if we record all the ways God answers prayer and shows up in our crises, we will see beyond the blob of green here, the speck of blue there. We will start to believe that there is more to each situation than we can imagine. That we're important, but not the *most* important thing. That we can trust that He's got our backs. And that He has no trouble connecting the dots.

✳ ✳ ✳

In my mind, the modern-day equivalent of pointillism is four-color process printing, known as CMYK. Most magazines, brochures, and newsletters are printed this way, with each element broken down into dots of four basic colors—cyan (blue), magenta (pink), yellow, and black (represented by the letter K). If you look through a magnifier, you will see the dots, but when you take it away or squint your eyes, your brain processes the dots into a blended image. Up close, you can see that the ink dots do not touch each other and that the colors do not continuously and smoothly blend together. The printed picture looks good hanging on the wall or sitting on your desk, and if the line screen is high (meaning there are a high number of dots per square inch) and the paper is good quality, the reproduction might look like the original work of art.

As long as you don't look too closely.

In 2008, after my mom heard the words *terminal cancer*, she was a different person. There were moments—glimpses—of the person she used to be. It sounded like her when I called several times a day. It looked like Mom next to me in the car when we went antiquing or out for lunch. But she was sad and scared, and the diagnosis changed her. Over time the disease did too—whether it was the cancer cells, the effects of the radiation to her brain, the tumors, the chemo, or later, the toxins her body was unable to secrete, her brain just wasn't the same.

We'd pretend nothing was different, that cancer hadn't bested us. In fact, we pretended so well that I think we forgot it was a pretense. We were trying to stay strong, wanting to enjoy every extra moment we had with her. It's true that those were gifts. But I was so desperate not to lose her that I didn't notice that she had faded into a pale reproduction of the woman I knew, not the original. That I had already lost a part of her.

I kept praying for healing. I didn't ever really expect complete and total healing, and in my core I knew God wasn't going to grant that, not this time. My heart wasn't strong enough to deal with that, though, so I doggedly ignored any evidence to the contrary and kept up a running pep talk, as if to convince myself. Pick up the kids (*Mom isn't gonna die*), run to the store for bread and eggs (*Mom surely isn't gonna die*), e-mail friends about Mom's latest test results (*Mom is* NOT *going to die—in spite of what all those websites tell me about statistics and symptoms*).

When Mom passed away in 2011, the tidal wave of grief rushed in, knocking me back against the wall. But there was an element to it that I hadn't expected—surprise. Shock. I couldn't believe it had really happened. And that it was so final.

I mean, really, how do you stand up and look God in the face (figuratively, of course) and shake your fist? Tell Him you are extremely *ticked off*? Tell Him you don't like the way He handled His business and you don't like the cards He dealt you and it's not fair and you want to hurt someone else, anyone, *anything* to keep from hurting this bad inside?

In my case, I didn't. I just pretended to keep serving Him. Eventually I even quit trying to pray. I was out of words, out of faith, and out of trust. My public faith was a farce. Yes, Mom had become a paler version of herself, changed by that horrible disease and its nearly-as-destructive treatments. But I was different too: Instead of a slightly faded version of the woman I was before, I became a complete imposter. A forgery.

On the surface, I may have looked the same. I posted prayers on Facebook, showed up at church, and thanked God publicly for each little moment of brightness. That all would have been fine if I'd believed it inside. But the thing about reproductions is that over time, colors fade. Edges curl. Papers warp. Once upon a time, the deception might have fooled people, but with the passing of time—or under close scrutiny—the truth becomes apparent to even the most casual observer. From a distance, the colors look like solid, continuous tones. But up close, you can see all the gaps between them.

Jesus knew of the dangers of hypocrisy.

"When you pray, don't be like the hypocrites who love
to pray publicly on street corners and in the synagogues
where everyone can see them. I tell you the truth, that
is all the reward they will ever get. But when you pray,
go away by yourself, shut the door behind you, and pray
to your Father in private. Then your Father, who sees
everything, will reward you."

MATTHEW 6:5-6

Jesus wasn't moved by public displays. But I'd put all my effort
into making a pretty picture for public viewing by placing little
colored dots lightly on the surface of the paper. Between those
dots, hidden in the gaps, was the real truth—that the woman
inside was furious and broken. And so alone. The God who had
always been beside her? Well, she wasn't sure she wanted Him
anymore. And she no longer had her mom to turn to. Yet all the
other people in her life still turned to God through the worst of it,
leaving only one conclusion: that she was the problem, not God.
That she had failed at this, too, and that He probably didn't want
her back.

Which didn't help.

I lost faith in the God who seemed to be unable (or worse,
unwilling) to help. The One who didn't stop me from having these
hard, hateful feelings. I never doubted that Mom was with Him. I
just resented Him for not caring about what I needed. Eventually I
began to wonder if, in fact, He really *could* heal, if He really could
comfort, or if that was something from long-ago Bible stories.

Fables maybe.

One night, in despair, I left the petulant, hateful child at the
door and went to Him in prayer, humble and reverent. I was

willing to face Him in spite of my shame if it meant I could have an answer. Willing to stop being mad if He'd show Himself to me again. I was fed up with all the well-meaning friends who talked about how, after so-and-so died, they kept seeing butterflies—or _____ (fill in the blank)—and they just *know* it's the spirit of so-and-so saying "I'm still here." As much as I wanted to find even one drop of comfort from believing that idea, I didn't. *God, please, help me understand. Are they right? Am I willfully ignoring these signs because I'm determined to be miserable? Because— truthfully?—I think she's really gone, for good. That's why my chest aches when I think of her. Why I still cry myself to sleep sometimes. Why I am still so broken. I need You, Lord, to show me what's true, to show me whatever I need to get past this place. To get back to You.*

Another night not long after that, I crawled into bed, exhausted, my defenses down. I peeled back another protective layer, sharing my true thoughts. *I miss her, Lord,* I whispered into the night. And a surety came over me, a silent voice so clear and strong and immediate that I couldn't deny it.

"SHE'S AS CLOSE AS I AM."

Oh, how that knocked the breath out of me.

I kept forgetting that God loves my mom, too. He did the best possible thing He could do for her—He let her walk away from the mental turmoil and physical pain, straight into His arms. And because she's with Him, eternally connected to Him, I can only find her again *in Him*. He's not withholding anything or punishing me. He hurts when I hurt. But in this world, people die.

In His Kingdom, though, that's not the end of the story.

It was then that I began to understand that my job was to paint something new. To walk away from my failings and to choose faith, to walk in a way that contradicted my emotions. To let go of the cheap imitation of a believer that I'd been and invest my time in creating something different. To let the ink dots of faith that made up my public face seep down into this new piece of paper, coloring it permanently. To believe that the gaps between dots aren't flaws, but that the empty spaces play a necessary role in the portrait of who I am.

I now understood the conundrum of Christian grief—that in order to draw close to the one you've lost, you must draw close to the One who allowed her to die. But from that moment on, I felt a stirring of faith. Over the next couple of years, it was a slow process of rebuilding. Oh, who am I kidding? It's not complete now, three years later. And now my dad has cancer too. I'm writing a book about seeing God, and now I'm being given a chance to live it out, to put it to the test. I could fight Him again, but I've already seen how that nearly destroyed me inside. I don't want to fight. I want His comfort. I want His grace. I want His forgiveness. I want His presence.

When you're fuming mad or broken-hearted, when you feel lost and abandoned and forsaken, God still leaves the decision in your hands—will you or won't you come to Him?

Faith is a choice, a daily, one-step-at-a-time decision to follow God. To believe in Him. To trust that His ways are best. To choose to believe that because of His supreme goodness, even when bad things happen, being with Him has to be better than being without. Even if I'm angry. Even if I'm hurt, wounded, raw. Even if I'm still reeling from the last tragedy I faced.

When you're fuming mad or brokenhearted, when you feel lost and abandoned and forsaken, He still leaves the decision in your hands—will you or won't you come to Him? Will you or won't you bring the pain with you, knowing that even though He didn't prevent it, He is the only cure for it? In Luke 7:21-23, it says

At that very time, Jesus cured many people of their
diseases, illnesses, and evil spirits, and he restored sight
to many who were blind. Then he told John's disciples,
"Go back to John and tell him what you have seen and
heard—the blind see, the lame walk, the lepers are cured,
the deaf hear, the dead are raised to life, and the Good
News is being preached to the poor. And tell him, 'God
blesses those who do not turn away *because of me.*'"
[emphasis added]

Turning away because of Jesus? Because I don't like the way
He handles His business? Jesus as a stumbling block—isn't that
backwards? No. No, it isn't. He's not surprised by how I feel.
He knew we wouldn't always like His answers—but He says we
will be blessed if we do not turn away because of them. Because
an encounter with Jesus always brings change, usually with unexpected results—"the blind see, the lame walk, the lepers are
cured, the deaf hear, the dead are raised to life."

The healing process is slow and still sometimes quite painful.
But I understand that the only way to heal is to seek my God
again. The only way to fullness is *through Him.* He is the only
balm, whether I like it or not. He is wholeness, completeness. He
is acceptance. He is my reality. He sees right through both the
cheap reproductions and the most sophisticated of forgeries. He
knows that the man-made dots are superficial and impermanent.

But when *He* paints them? He is the only One who can take
a bunch of disconnected, messy dots and transform them into a
vibrant, living work of art.

PRAYER PALETTE

Faith isn't the ability to believe long and far into the misty future. It's simply taking God at His Word and taking the next step.
~JONI EARECKSON TADA

EXAMINE THE DOTS. Jot down a list of times when you felt that God was far away, or focus on one particular time in your life when you were too angry, defeated, disappointed, or sad to pray. Or think of a time when you felt God failed you. Write a couple of paragraphs about that time—how you felt, what you did. Then skip a couple of lines and rewrite the scenario from God's point of view, as though He is telling the story to you.

WRITE A SCREENPLAY (a short one). Taking the situation(s) you wrote down above, try to tell the story in the form of a movie script. Include God as one of the characters. Don't forget to notice where He was, what He was doing, what He would have said if this screenplay were being filmed.

LET YOURSELF "GO THERE." Sit quietly by yourself. Ask God to be with you. Write down how angry, hurt, upset, alone, or betrayed you've felt by God, or by a church, or by someone you love. Then, if you have a safe place to do so, burn the paper. (Use a paper shredder if you don't have a fireplace or other safe place to do this.) While you watch the paper being destroyed, ask God to consume your negative feelings, the hurts you've carried with you, to burn them up completely and replace them with an assurance that He will never leave you. Ask Him to help you forgive and to see that He really was there, that He really does know best. And know that God is bigger than any of our fears. "Does it mean he no longer loves us if we have trouble or calamity, or are persecuted, or hungry, or destitute, or in danger, or threatened with death? . . . Nothing can ever separate us from God's love" (Romans 8:35, 38). He can handle the truth of how you feel. And He can heal the broken places. Just allow Him in.

Symbols express all kinds of emotions and ideas.

CHAPTER 18

PRAYER PROMPTS

(SYMBOLS)

Symbols are miracles we have recorded into language.

S. KELLEY HARRELL

Getting to wear thrift-store trench coats and carry an elaborately decorated sketchbook weren't the only perks of being an art major. In one of my design studios, we got to play games. Loosely based on the games *Pictionary* and *Win, Lose or Draw*, our game consisted of selecting a slip of paper and then going to the board to draw the phrase written on it by using symbols, sketches, and gestures. Anything but actual written words.

Goofing off? Maybe a little. But with a purpose. Symbols are simple shapes used to represent an idea or object—easily recognizable, they correspond to specific ideas. Think about the symbols used on road signs (railroad crossings, merging) and warning labels (skull and crossbones, a red circle with a diagonal line across it). As a graphic designer, I spend quite a bit of time designing logos. Some are crafted from nothing but type, but most have an icon or symbol with the words. Truly iconic logos from some of the more prominent retail companies are recognizable even without their names. The Target bull's-eye (my happy place). Nike's swoosh (people who run faster than I). The stylized green circular siren on every Starbucks door (caffeine!). Apple's, well, apple.

At its heart, logo design is about reducing a complicated concept to its essence, representing an idea in a clear, stylized way. For all of you who were afraid to pick up this book because you "can't even draw a straight line," remember—straight lines are not required. Drawing skill is not required either. When you play this game, you have nothing to copy and no time to sketch carefully. You just start moving your marker. Quick lines and gestures. You break words apart ("home" and "town" for "hometown"). You look for sound-alike words. You have to get creative.

If you're still feeling like the idea of symbols is a little beyond you, let me remind you that you've been doing this your whole life. Draw a smiley face on a scrap of paper. I'm serious. Quickly! Are you done yet? Okay, look closely at it. Who does it look like? Abe

Lincoln? JLo? Your uncle Eddie? Unless someone has exceptionally chubby features, this circle with a couple of dots and a curved line probably doesn't look anything like a real person. But everyone "sees" it as a face. When our society started incorporating them into e-mails—:-)—people started experimenting, and now we recognize a boatload of variations on that theme—;) :-D :{ =]. We've trained our minds so when we see the symbol, our mind translates it from a series of punctuation marks into an idea. Happy. Laughter. Funny. Sad. Or whatever it needs to be at any given moment.

Several years ago, my friend Lisa wrote an essay titled, "Whenever I See John Wayne, I Remember to Pray for You." The idea was this: Assign objects to represent different people in your life, and use those objects as visual reminders to pray. Lisa's husband, Mike, is a big John Wayne fan, so whenever she sees an image of John Wayne—on TV, on a DVD case at Target, in a magazine—she prays for Mike. My friend Peggy loves chocolate chip cookies. When Lisa sees chocolate chip cookies, she says a prayer for Peggy. (And then enjoys one in Peggy's honor.)

Most of us probably already connect certain objects with a friend, child, spouse, or parent. Using these symbols as prayer markers is elevating them from a fleeting thought into a God-bound prayer.

Most of us probably already connect certain objects with a friend, child, spouse, or parent. Using these symbols as prayer markers is just taking those passing impressions to the next level—elevating them from a fleeting thought into a God-bound prayer. The idea is to choose something to connect to the person you want to remember, something you're likely to see or hear during the week. You can choose a sound (a teakettle whistling or a specific song), a person (real, fictional, or cartoon), a color or object (a Harley-Davidson motorcycle, a train). You can pray for each of your family members as you fold their laundry.

Bill, a pastor and friend of Lisa's, tells a story about helping to train elders in a small church. He challenged the group to pray consistently and specifically for their pastor. The group's pastor, who had very little hair and a hearty sense of humor, pointed to his balding head and said, "Every time you pass a bowling alley, remember to pray for me!"

Pray without ceasing.
1 THESSALONIANS 5:17, KJV

Many of you will be familiar with this Scripture. When I read this, I nod to myself, grasping the validity of the idea and recognizing the need for constant prayer. But in practice, I fall short. Frankly, I fall so short you probably would never guess that I was even trying to aspire to this. When I first learned this verse, I felt overwhelmed by the impossibility of achieving it. How could I pray *all the time*? I have three kids. And a job. A husband, a family, friends, dust bunnies under my bed, and a ring in my bathtub. Books to read. Chocolate to eat.

Lisa enlightened me again. "Think of it as a radio playing music in the background. It's always on."

Is anyone out there old enough to remember the days of dial-up Internet access? Sometimes it took a while for the mystical connection to take place—you would start the process, wait for the series of tones and beeps, go brush your teeth or load the dishwasher or check the mailbox—and then sit down to check your e-mail. (And after the initial connection, while it loaded at superslow speeds, you'd still have time to throw your kids' toys into the toy box.) Still, I marveled at this wonderful technology. Now, most of us take for granted the fact that our devices are always on.

As I ride in my car through our small downtown, four or five Wi-Fi networks pop up on my phone. And when I don't have Wi-Fi, I still have the ability to connect to the Internet at any time from any place through my smartphone and data plan. Easy access, nearly instant access, all the time.

But God is bigger than the Internet. He's always there, always available, always working, no software or data plan upgrade required. Keep up a running dialogue in the background. *Thank You for this sunny day, Lord. . . . Fill that ambulance with Your presence. Let them feel You. . . . Please help Katie on her chemistry exam this morning. . . . Help me stop worrying and start to focus—I have a lot to do today. . . . Ooh, those cookies look good—Peggy would love them. Speak to her as she prepares tonight's Bible study lesson. . . . Thank You for protecting me—please help that truck driver stay awake and in his own lane. Thank You for the long hours he puts in to make a living, transporting things that people need. . . . Oh, what a beautiful sunset—You amaze me with Your creation. Such variety. . . . Dwell in the midst of that conversation, Lord. Help that woman to hear Your words through her friend. Let her drink You in like that coffee.*

When you talk to Him all the time, the connection stays open. And then, when crisis hits, when a friend is miscarrying or a parent becomes ill or an acquaintance walks into rehab or the fire department is unable to salvage your home, you don't have to wait for the *bomp bomp ba donk* of the modem connecting. He's already there. The line is already open. No preparation needed. No hesitation, no warming up, no easing into it. You're right there.

And so is He.

* * *

A few months after college, I was working as an art director at an ad agency in Indianapolis. Once in a while, the four art directors escaped to lunch at the same time. I remember sitting in Wendy's as Bryan compared the chicken sandwich on his tray with the one on the window-sized poster. They were both identifiable as food, and yes, even as chicken sandwiches, but that's where the similarities ended. The limp, lopsided sandwich he unwrapped looked like a poor cousin to the poster child. Since we produced marketing materials on a daily basis, I think we were particularly offended by such misleading advertising.

Now I'm not picking on Wendy's. The same could be said of any other restaurant. Apparently, it's nearly impossible to have a glistening piece of meat that isn't greasy—and in Indiana, at least, you're just not going to get a ripe tomato slice (unless it's from a friend's garden during the month of August). We could still recognize it for what it was, but the sandwich on the tray certainly was lacking. That's the reality we live with every day. Our experiences often don't live up to our expectations. At lunch, or in prayer.

When you pray, you may approach God with certain expectations, certain symbols in your mind, whether you verbalize them or not. I personally believe it's okay to tell God what you're hoping for, but I've learned over the years that since He usually has much better ideas than I do, it's best to include a disclaimer. *Lord, knowing what I know, this seems like the best idea to me. But You know far more, and Your plans are perfect. Don't let my request for this get in the way of the right answer. I want what You want.*

It is frightening to pray that. Addie Zierman writes, "It is the tender heart of my greatest doubts, my biggest fears about God. Namely, that I could pray my little heart out for a certain outcome, a particular miracle, and in his terrible Goodness, God might do exactly the opposite."[28]

It's true that He might. We've discussed some of the crazy ways God answers prayer. Even when the answer isn't upside down, it may not exactly be right-side up, either. But it's always right.

Andrea, a dear friend and mentor of mine, had the guts to go ahead and ask for something crazy. As her father reached his nineties, he was still pastoring a church. Andrea watched from a distance as his congregation dwindled down to around ten members. He clung tightly to the role he'd had for many years, but he wasn't able mentally to lead the way he had in the past. She desperately wanted her dad to be able to go out with his head held high, to retire with pride from a long and faithful career serving the Lord.

If it had been me, I might have prayed for someone new to come along whom her father could take under his wing and groom for leadership. Or for him to find a new ministry. Or for him to change. Or something. I don't know.

Andrea, though, prayed what is perhaps the most surprising prayer I've heard. She knew that her father was alienating people with his words, that he was becoming more harsh and set in his ways, offending many. She knew that he had done a lot of good in his years in ministry and that his heart was in the right place, even if his mind was not. She prayed that God would send foreigners to that church, nonnative speakers who would not know what he was saying.

And in no time, around seventy-five or so Romanian immigrants arrived in that specific town in Arkansas. They filled the church. Only one of them understood English, and Andrea's father didn't know Romanian, but the immigrants wanted to build a community there. They rented the building to hold their foreign-language services. Andrea's father's involvement in the services wasn't needed anymore since he didn't speak their language, and he retired with his head held high.

A crazy prayer, and a crazy answer. But it seemed to be just the right one.

In our symbol-laden culture, we expect our lives, bodies, and faith to be as simple, beautiful, airbrushed, thin, mouthwatering, terrifying, bold, extreme, or enormous as the idealized examples filling the airwaves. It's not enough to be pretty. We want to be nearly anorexic, streaks of gray hidden beneath hair dye, clad in just the right designer jeans (that look like jeans we've worn for twenty years, only better), revealing just the right amount of cleavage, and wearing a glittering rock on our left hand. It's not enough to like our jobs and feel we're making a difference. We long to be featured in an *Entrepreneur* magazine article as the youngest-ever billionaire. We dream of seeing the story of our against-all-odds rise to fame stay at the top of the *New York Times* Best Sellers list indefinitely. We measure success by the tangibles, not the intangibles.

> *We measure success by the tangibles, not the intangibles. God's measure of success is different. We have our expectations set too high for ourselves—and not high enough for God.*

Being a good enough mom doesn't cut it—Pinterest and Facebook inundate us all day long with picture-perfect meals we envy and elaborate handmade birthday party decorations we wish we had time to make. They seem all the more impressive because the only time we can slow down enough to look at the pictures is in the drive-through lane on our way to the next baseball practice. It's not enough to have a quiet, solid faith or to lead by example—instead, we think we have to raise millions for children in Haiti or grow our church membership to four digits. And then five.

Jesus saw these same desires two thousand years ago.

"Don't store up treasures here on earth, where moths eat them and rust destroys them, and where thieves break in and steal. Store your treasures in heaven, where moths and rust cannot destroy, and thieves do not break in and steal.

Wherever your treasure is, there the desires of your heart will also be."

MATTHEW 6:19-21

God's measure of success is different from everyone else's. So why do we expect our less-than-perfect selves to perform at such high levels and then not expect the perfect God to perform miraculous feats? We have our expectations set too high for ourselves—and not high enough for God.

Let go of some of your expectations, both in your daily life and in your prayer life. Don't try to force God into your picture, somewhere around the edges. Instead, hand over the pencil and ask Him to show you how He would draw your life. The answer He gives you will look different from the answer He gives me—but they're both chicken sandwiches. And His will come with a juicy red tomato.

PRAYER PALETTE

The soul . . . may have many symbols with which it reaches toward God. ~ANYA SETON

SYMBOLISM WORKSHEET. List the names of the people most important—or most present—in your life. On the right, list anything that reminds you of that person. Think about foods, movies, books, or colors they like; how you met them; hobbies or interests you have in common; items they collect or own. When you're done, go back through and circle the one that is the most obvious, easy-to-remember symbol for that person. From now on, when you see it, pray for him or her.

PRAYER CALENDAR. Fill in the upcoming month's squares on a calendar with names of people who come to mind. Every time you glance at the calendar, pray for the person listed on that day.

PRAYER PLAYLIST. Make a playlist of songs that remind you of people close to you. Then play it while you work or clean. As each song begins to play, pray for the person you connect with that song. These don't have to be spiritual songs. My playlist goes something like this: Peggy loves Jimmy Buffet, so "Cheeseburger in Paradise" makes me think of her. Bobby likes to play One Republic's "Secrets" on the piano. Michael W. Smith's "This Is the Air I Breathe" is a song I listened to when my six-year-old neighbor, Henry, was fighting cancer. Mom loved the musical *Mamma Mia*, and Dad loves Billy Joel. Each song provides a reminder of a particular person and prompts me to pray.

Simplicity can elicit a sense of serenity.

CHAPTER 19

THE PURITY OF PRAYER

(SIMPLICITY AND MINIMALISM)

The ability to simplify means to eliminate the unnecessary so that the necessary may speak.

HANS HOFMANN

Prayer, in its simplest form, is communion with God. Raw, bare, honest, vulnerable communication. Words, thoughts, ions, dust motes traveling between us in the light. Thoughts, love, hope. Touch, the sense of an invisible presence. Connection.

And isn't that also what art is? An attempt to connect with the person on the other side of the artwork?

When I joined the Catholic church twenty-four years ago, at the time in my life in which I first felt that nudge, that pull toward God, I used to leave Mass longing to bring that feeling with me. To have the music at home. To find there what I found at church. It was a new concept, an idea I'd never considered.

What I loved so much then was the power of my words joined with others. The swell of our prayers were not vain repetitions; they were joined together, our spirits blended with the super-natural God. Words, praises, petitions met in the air and surged upward and onward, exponentially expanded, forever changed. I kept thinking, *I'm not in this alone. I'm part of something bigger.* In that church, with the exposed dark wooden rafters and sunlight flitting through the colorful painted glass, with Jesus hanging on the cross over altars of incense and robed priests intoning bless-ings, I could feel it. The power of it. The enormity and magnitude of God. There were just a few hundred in our congregation, yet all over the world, in different languages and buildings and styles, God's people came together through the power of shared prayer.

Many years later, at Grace & Mercy, I still saw the power of group prayer, even if the form—spontaneous, emotional, and without ritual—was completely different. I also learned, from the teachings at my church and on my own, that there is immense power in solitary prayer as well. Both are valuable. Both have changed me. It is exhilarating to pray with others, whether recit-ing formal liturgy or gathered in a circle at the altar, laying on hands and petitioning urgently on someone else's behalf. Those instances, with arms extended and emotion flowing, are beautiful and almost decorative in their indulgence; whereas quiet times alone with God are simplicity in its purest form. When everything is stripped away, there is nothing else. No distraction, no tug on your time or attention.

No place to hide from the truth.

Minimalism is a form of art that sets out to expose the essence of a subject by eliminating all nonessential forms. The simplest and fewest elements are meant to achieve the maximum effect. In practical terms, all distractions are eliminated. By concentrating on just one principle (such as symmetry), an artist can create a strong point of interest, making it clear what we are looking at. Simplicity in art is an attempt to portray emotion by paring down an image to its essence.

> *It is in the simple that we find the profound. Simplicity is about finding more, not less. You might even say that's upside down.*

When we talk about simplicity, people may automatically conclude it means *absence*—of luxury or sophistication, of intelligence or embellishment. They think simplicity means austere, bare, empty. But it is in the simple that we find the profound. Simplicity is about finding *more*, not less.

You might even say that's upside down.

In 1903, American novelist Frank Norris published an essay titled "Simplicity in Art," about shopping for a silver soup ladle. After viewing several ornate pieces of silver, the salesman showed him one more. Norris wrote,

> He brought out a ladle that was as plain and as unadorned as the unclouded sky—and about as beautiful. Of all the others this was the most to my liking. But the price! . . . It was

nearly double the cost of any of the rest. And when I asked why, the salesman said:

"You see, in this highly ornamental ware the flaws of the material don't show, and you can cover up a blow-hole or the like by wreaths and beading. But this plain ware has got to be the very best. Every defect is apparent."[29]

Let your words be few.

ECCLESIASTES 5:2

I find it hard to write unless I'm by myself. Having my kids or husband in the room creates an invisible tug on me. A part of my mind remains tuned to their potential needs. I struggle with focusing, letting go, dropping my barriers, and allowing myself to be vulnerable. I see the same phenomenon in prayer. As much as I love praying with a group, praying alone is a totally different experience, essential and valuable.

Shh. Eyes closed, doors locked, silence undulating in waves all around. God in attendance. All activity hushes, and He waits. This is simplicity in prayer. This is when you will hear, in the silence. This is when you will see, with your eyes closed. Because as beautiful or powerful as corporate prayer can be, it's like the ladle—it's possible, beneath all the noise and fanfare, to hide a flaw. To let one of many elements drown out your still small voice, to miss a *lack* because of all the *plenty.*

Think back to your dating days. (I've been married a long time, so I'm really digging into the memory banks here.) If you didn't like the boy, you would ensure you were never left alone with him. On the other hand, if you really liked someone, you didn't have much of a problem being alone with him. You longed for it and probably even crafted elaborate ruses to orchestrate a few moments in private.

When I was in college, a friend I adored but had never dated came back a few months after his graduation. My roommate, Clarice, knew how much I wanted to see him and that he'd only be staying a couple of hours. So that afternoon, when he walked in, she sat down with us and made awkward small talk, even though I was willing her to leave the entire time. When he said he had to go, Clarice seized her opportunity too. I could have killed her. I just knew if she had left us alone, he would have kissed me. (Apparently Clarice had wisely appointed herself as my protector.) Sometimes I find myself using all the tools of prayer—Bible, journal, worship music—as distractions, protection against being real and true and open and vulnerable. They crowd out intimacy with God as well as what results from those intimate times: God bringing my flaws into the light.

It's a legitimate fear. When we spend time alone in prayer, God blows off the chaff.[30] Shines His light on our darkness,[31] exposing all. He separates what is valuable from what is worthless. If you recall, Jesus chastised the Pharisees for their public displays of faith, not because they were *public* but because they were *shows*.[32] Performances masking the truth.

All prayer is good and valid and helpful—whether tilted, upside down, sideways, or right-side up—as long as it's real. It only needs to come from a purity of purpose and a desire to seek Him. But, even within that definition, there are many different ways to approach prayer. Some you'll use your whole life. Some will seem to work better during different seasons. If the ones mentioned here do not fit your personality or situation, get creative and find your own approach.

> *All prayer is good and valid and helpful, as long as it's real. It only needs to come from a purity of purpose and a desire to seek God.*

Margaret Feinberg wrote in *Wonderstruck* that one year she felt God asking her to give up prayer for Lent. *How can that be?* she wondered, but she cautiously did what she felt He was asking. She sensed that she shouldn't give up prayer completely, just long, elaborate prayers. When all the ornamental verbiage was stripped away, she discovered that she tapped into pure power and true meaning. It wasn't *easier* to simplify, but *harder*. It required more discipline, more focus, more purpose. There are different ways to do this. Margaret limited herself to three words. As she eliminated the excess, the fundamental meaning of the words she prayed expanded within her soul. Applying a similar idea to my own prayers, *Please heal Katie's migraines* becomes, simply, *Heal*. And *Please give my husband the promotion he deserves* becomes, simply, *Work*.

Anne Lamott wrote a book professing that even the most complex prayers can be simplified into a single word that encompasses everything we need to say. She suggests that all of our needs and requests can be summed up in these three short prayers: *help*, *thanks*, and *wow*.[33]

What these women and others have discovered is that it doesn't take a great number of words to communicate with God and to be changed by the process. There's no advantage to being verbose or ostentatious. Just be open. Honest. Next time you are alone with God, give *less* a try.

Worship

Maybe your prayer shouldn't be prayer at all. Sometimes unadorned, heartfelt worship is the best thing you can offer God. A few years ago, I attended a meeting. There were eight of us in the room, mostly pastors, all people whose faith guides their lives. The man leading the meeting opened with prayer and then asked us to join him in a worship song. The harmony was inspired, the song anointed, the emotions pure, the mood intimate and lovely. It was so beautiful I got goose bumps on my arms. There was no music or microphones. We weren't dressed in our Sunday best. We were sitting around a table, notepads open, coffee cooling in the cups beside us. The moment was more intensely spiritual than most of my experiences in the sanctuary, surrounded by a hundred other people. Because on this day, the worship was pared down to the basics. It was real, genuine, true. Nothing more than our hearts reaching for our God.

When you sit down to pray, when you feel worship bubbling forth, or when you're desperate for help or relief, don't waste time with gadgets and gimmicks. There is no need to spend half an hour searching for just the right song on iTunes. Don't wait until you can call your friend to pray with you or lose time looking for a particular passage of Scripture to get you started. Turn off the TV, leave the lawn unmowed, and close in with the Lord. Reflect on who He is, what He's done, and all the ways you've seen Him. Don't ask for a thing. Thank Him for what He's already given and done for you. Praise Him for who He is. Tell Him how you feel. Sing, dance, write, or lie facedown on the floor. Bow your head in the quiet or speak to Him out loud. Whatever you feel, whatever He inspires. If you're nervous about someone else seeing you, close your curtains and lock the front door. Because only one Person matters. He won't laugh at you, no matter how silly you feel. He'll be right there with you, inhabiting the silence and filling the emptiness.

PRAYER PALETTE

Simplicity of shape does not necessarily equate with simplicity of experience. ~ ROBERT MORRIS

CHOOSE ONE WORD. A popular approach is to prayerfully select one word to use as a focus all year long. It might be *seek, hope, renew, forgive, serve.* Ask God to show you how to apply the word every day. Journey with Him to discover what this looks like when it's put into practice. My friend Jen asked God if He had anything—a word, a concept, a verse—that He wanted her to focus on for the year. The same word kept coming to the surface. *Pause.* She wrote:

> *Okay, Lord. Pause? That's not exactly the word I was looking for. I was thinking of something more glamorous . . . like kindness, or mercy, or grace. But pause? What am I supposed to do with that?* And that's the point. . . . He doesn't want me to do anything with it. He wants me to pause. Wait. Stop. Think. Reflect. Look around. Listen. Observe.

> *Pause.*

The more time I've spent praying, studying the Word, and looking back through my journals and study notes, the more I realize that I've been doing a lot. A lot of ministry, a lot of teaching, a lot of mothering, a lot of counseling . . . a lot of activity. It isn't that I think any of the things I've done have been done with wrong motives or out of step with God, but it's been a busy, busy season. Really busy. Sometimes you need to stop and just . . . breathe.

That year, as Jen slowed down and sat at the feet of God, she listened. Waited. Heard. Grew. And during that time she discovered—surprise!—that she was pregnant with her fifth child, a baby she named Selah (which means "pause"). Having Selah reminded Jen to focus on her family, to remember what's important.

Take time to wait on the Lord and see what He has for you, because even if it's not what you're expecting, you may just find out that it's exactly what you need.

MEDITATE. Choose one Scripture, and meditate on it in prayer. Be especially aware of God's presence as you play with it, cherish it, find its nuances and hidden meanings. Research it, look up the words in a concordance, find other related Scriptures. Savor it, examine it, ponder it, and ingest it. Don't hurry through a checklist of verses to memorize, but find one, just one, and make it your own.

BASK IN THE SILENCE. It's really that simple: Quiet your mind and focus on Him. Feel yourself opening your heart, your soul—and direct it all toward God. Prepare to receive. Contemplate. Listen. A swirl of thoughts, a vortex of emotion, a rush of peace. His presence, real and encompassing and alive, will be there in the silence.

Keep your tools always within reach.

CHAPTER 20

BRINGING THE FISH

(AN ARTIST'S TOOLS)

There are no rules, just tools.

GLENN VILPPU, ANIMATOR

221

A quill pen filled with black ink leaves a different mark than a chalky, square pastel. Want bold shadows that are easily blended? Charcoal is a good choice. Translucent, transparent, vivid, subtle, blended, harsh, thick, delicate—each need requires a separate tool. Art supply stores stock aisle upon aisle of brushes, paints, pencils, chalk, papers, and inks—hundreds and hundreds of different items, in all colors, widths, weights, materials. When I go in without a specific project in mind, the sheer variety overwhelms me, and I might leave the best art supply store in the world with nothing more than a lime-green Sharpie. I don't even know where to start when I don't have a specific need in mind. But when I have a particular project to complete, there are no limits. Once the need is identified, I know just what tool to grab.

Don't limit your definition to only the most obvious tools such as brushes, a palette, and solvent. Just as important are the canvas on which you're painting and the easel that props it up. The margins, the edges, the picture hanger. The techniques you use, the subject matter, the knowledge through which you evaluate it.

One tool isn't enough for a lifetime of prayer, just as one tool would not satisfy an artist for life. Combine them, mix them—maybe discover something new.

When you pray, use whatever you have—all that you know. Whatever works for you. But when you get tired of hearing yourself pray the same thing again and again, and perhaps start to feel a little disappointed in a God who would listen to such stale words and not just answer you to be done with it, step back and evaluate. The best way to find out how your tools work is to experiment.

Do you need to simplify a complex situation? Try the grid method, grabbing hold of one square at a time on your way to seeing the big picture. Want God to give you a definite answer to an important question? Present the situation to Him in prayer, recount all the ways He's already helped you, and then listen. Leave a little white space so you can hear it when it comes. Or start "sketching" in a prayer journal, and see where the words take you. Feel like you're too focused on yourself? Try praying upside down. One tool isn't enough for a lifetime of prayer, just as one tool would not satisfy an artist for life.

In order to achieve the greatest potential, though, you must master your tools. They are the vehicles that will take you to where you want to be. Like any artist, you should figure out what technique is appropriate for each need. Try using your tools in new ways. Combine them, mix them—maybe discover something new. As Napoleon Hill wrote, "Do not wait. The time will never be 'just right.' Start where you stand, work with whatever tools you may have at your command, and better tools will be found as you go along."[34]

Those tools are God's gift to you. Share them. Rejoice in them. Use them.

> "There's a young boy here with five barley loaves and two fish. But what good is that with this huge crowd?"
> JOHN 6:9

We hear these Bible stories told and retold whenever our resources don't stretch far enough and when we're in need of some kind of miraculous provision. Even those of us who had limited exposure to church in our youth can probably call to mind the illustrated scene from a story Bible. Heaping baskets of fish and piles of loaves, people standing and sitting on hills with Jesus facing them. One day Jesus fed 4,000 people with seven loaves and a few fish, and another time He fed 5,000 from just five loaves and two fish.

The beauty of these stories is the point that God is not limited in His ability to provide. He always brings more than enough. There is always increase when God is involved. And there are always leftovers.

Knowing this story, though, doesn't necessarily make believing it any easier. No matter how strong you think your faith is, you will have times when you doubt. When you wonder if what God gives you will really be enough. If God will intervene in time (or at all). You might be thinking, *Maybe somehow I'm exempt. Maybe I don't deserve it. Maybe He's too busy to notice. Maybe this is too trivial to bother God with.*

And the heart of our deepest fears: *Maybe He doesn't care.*

If you always knew the outcome, you wouldn't need faith. If you've been fortunate enough to notice God's provision in the past, it's a little easier to hold on, whether He came through for you or for someone else—because, in theory, you have seen with your own eyes that it's possible. But even if you think you believe with your whole heart, the skeptic inside your brain may be shouting, as mine does, *Wait! Hold on a second! How in the world do I get there from here? How do I make the leap to thousands of loaves when all I have in front of me are a few crumbs?*

Guess what? You don't have to. The answer lies not in what you have in front of you, but what God has in front of Him. Before Jesus worked miracles, He took stock of what He had to work with, what was really there. Which brings us to the often-overlooked, and in my opinion, most critical fact in this story: *Someone had to provide the fish.*

The young boy who offered his lunch didn't create the miracle. God could have done it without him. I believe God regularly creates something from nothing—a faithful, loving marriage where there was formerly no trust. Peace in the midst of black-clothed mourners at a funeral. More often, He works with what we initially bring to Him, with what we stretch forward in our hands as an offering, whether literally or symbolically.

The more we're willing to let go of, the more He multiplies. We plant a seed of giving by paying tithes and offerings and donating to charitable organizations. When we put aside our egos and desires, we make room for His presence. To see God accomplish above and beyond that which we can even imagine, we must offer Him our whole selves—bodies, hearts, minds, and souls—and mean it when we ask Him to use us. Because when we do, God *will* multiply. He *will* create. He *will* increase—starting with exactly what you offered Him. Don't ever fall into the trap of believing that God won't come through because of your current (or past) failings. Or that what you have to offer isn't enough. He's already given you everything you need to see Him, to find Him, to reach Him.

> *Don't ever fall into the trap of believing that God won't come through because of your current (or past) failings. Or that what you have to offer isn't enough.*

Stand tall and open your hands. Speak toward the heavens: *Lord, I may not have much, but I offer You my fish. Multiply this offering. I believe.*

That is what we're doing with these upside-down prayer techniques. We're bringing the fish. We're opening our toolboxes and taking stock of the resources we have available, then waiting in expectation for Him to create something really magnificent.

Here's the funny thing about God: He rarely draws our answers in straight lines. Yet the answers still come. His solutions often seem convoluted, confusing, maybe even down-to-the-last-second crazy. We cling to stories of miraculous solutions. The check (or tax refund or bonus or raise) arrives the day the bill you thought you couldn't pay is due. Doctors mention terrifying words like *aneurysm* and *cancer* and *inoperable,* so you have the tests done and pray, and suddenly, although the doctors can't explain it, the condition is gone or the symptoms weren't what they seemed. We lose a job and panic, worried about how to provide for our families, but then another, better opportunity presents itself and we wonder why we didn't leave the old job sooner. God always delivers—somehow, some way.

On the other hand, it's disappointing, sometimes devastating, when His answer isn't the one you'd hoped for—when the cancer comes back, or your spouse doesn't return home—or when His timing doesn't match yours. God's ways are not our ways (and I am grateful for that).

> "My thoughts are nothing like your thoughts," says the
>   LORD.
>   "And my ways are far beyond anything you could
>   imagine.
> For just as the heavens are higher than the earth,
>   so my ways are higher than your ways
>   and my thoughts higher than your thoughts."
> ISAIAH 55:8-9

Some answers may thrill your soul, and others may break your heart. He knows what He's doing, even if we can't see it yet. Even if we can't fathom that any good could possibly exist in the midst of suffering or sorrow, it does. God sees that what is tragic or heartbreaking—what feels like the end to us—really is not the end of the story. He promises "he will never leave you nor forsake you,"[35] which means He will always stay beside you as you face whatever comes your way.

Because He is *always* in the answer. And He doesn't make mistakes.

A life spent making mistakes is not only more honorable,
but more useful than a life spent doing nothing.

GEORGE BERNARD SHAW, *HEARTBREAK HOUSE*

I think you've probably figured this out by now, but I've always been a geek. The ultimate proof: I did algebra homework in ink. I liked the challenge—could I get them all right the first time? Could I keep the columns of numbers and equations lined up nice and neat? I think I mainly wanted to show off, to prove that I knew what I was doing.

In the years since, I've come to a very different conclusion. Life isn't algebra, and I am wrong quite often. One small way I know this is because the erasers on the ends of all my pencils are gone.

I'm not ashamed of that. Instead, I celebrate the fact that someone had the foresight to know I would make mistakes, so they placed the eraser in a handy spot. We've talked about ways to draw, ways to see and paint and sketch. But in reality, the eraser is just as important a tool for drawing as the pencil. It gets rid of what doesn't belong so we can focus on what does.

God draws in ink because He knows what He's doing—but He knew *we'd* mess up. As Jon Acuff writes,

Jesus tells Simon: "And *when* you have turned back, strengthen your brothers." That's it. Those are nine really simple words, but they demand a second look. . . . Jesus is . . . saying: And *when* you fail. And *when* you sin. And *when* you blow it and sell me out like a common thief. And *when* you literally and physically turn your back on me. And *when* you ruin it all. *When you turn back.*[36]

God gave us the eraser we need, and it's called *repentance*. If we repent (turn away) from the things we've done wrong, God will forgive us. Our sins (failings, mistakes, poor judgment, and bad choices) are gone. Just like that. When God forgives us, it means our mistakes are blotted out, erased, as if they were never there in the first place. He no longer sees that mistake again, big or small. There are no indentations in the paper, no places where the paper is worn thin. They are gone. When you pray, ask Him to forgive you for the things you shouldn't have done. And once He has, once they are rubbed out, don't draw them in again. Instead, let God fill that space with something new.

My friend Elizabeth told me once about painting on a new, nonporous watercolor paper. The sections where she had the least mastery—where the paint practically took on a life of its own and she had no choice but to relinquish control—were the most interesting. An artist can reach a certain level of skill with the materials she uses but will inevitably have to accept what happens, even if it is unpredictable or unexpected. Sometimes a mistake ends up being beautiful. In art, it's often called the happy accident. As your skill grows, you learn ways to fix those mistakes—or, more exciting, how to transform that mistake into something even better. Don't give up when things don't go your way. Work with it. Yield your logic and follow your gut. It might be the best thing that ever happened to your art (and your prayers), because the so-called *mistakes* you make may ultimately show you the most about our God and His grace.

✳ ✳ ✳

Whether you make mistakes or think you're doing everything right, sometimes things just don't come together like you want. For some of us, it's more fun to buy new running shoes than it is to run. More fun to pick out colorful office supplies than to sort through stacks of paper and put them in some kind of order. More fun to buy the economics textbook than trudge through forty-three chapters.

It's certainly easier to buy devotional books and t-shirts than to dedicate yourself to regular one-on-one time with God. To overcome your doubts, face your fears, risk disappointment, and really, truly come to know Him.

Having the tool is different than *using* the tool. And with prayer, *using* the tools is what matters. You can know all about prayer, but if you don't actually pray, you won't see results.

I recently enrolled in a drawing class to brush up on my technique, and I was shocked by how much my skills had atrophied. It takes practice—ongoing, regular practice—to obtain good results. Even so, you might face obstacles. A broken tool. A loss of inspiration. Maybe the fruit used in the still life molds and rots from sitting too long in the light. That doesn't mean the work isn't worthwhile or that you did something wrong or even that the result itself is inherently bad.

Consider this: Maybe you're not ready for the answer yet. A quarter is a deadly choking hazard for a baby, but for a ten-year-old it's the means to obtain the gummy, blue sticky-hand from the vending machine at Steak 'n Shake. To a teenager, it's one-third of the cost of a 32-ounce cup of Mountain Dew—a small but helpful part of the total. The same object has a different value for each person. To some adults, it's hardly worth stooping down to pick it up off the floor.

The other thing to remember about tools is this: What Michelangelo could do with a pencil is a far greater thing than what most of us can do. You and I won't have the same results. I may sketch a soft, shaky, tentative line while you boldly capture the essence of someone's personality in dark, confident strokes. Our styles will be as different as our personalities. In the end, though, we've both attempted to communicate what we see. We've both created art.

Unlike art, talent has nothing to do with success in prayer. Success is, quite simply, doing it. God is waiting, and He already knows what tools will make the right kind of mark in your situation.

PRAYER PALETTE

Have thy tools ready. God will find thee work. ~CHARLES KINGSLEY

TAKE STOCK. The reason I provided the Prayer Palettes at the end of most chapters is to help you put each prayer tool to use. Right now, take a few minutes to review what's in your toolbox. But don't stop there. Pick up a tool—any tool—and get busy. As you use them, you may notice that many of the techniques apply to other types of prayers too. Feel free to switch them around and try them in different ways. On the TV series *MacGyver*, the title character was a master of ingenuity. Give him whatever random objects were within reach—a screwdriver, orange juice, a shoelace, or a battery—and he could improvise a bomb or build a contraption to unlock a door or otherwise save the day.

And that's just on TV. What the human mind can imagine. There are no limits to what our unlimited God can do with the tools we put in front of Him.

Each artist expresses his or her style in a different way.

CHAPTER 21

FINDING YOUR OWN STYLE

(THE ARTIST'S PROCESS)

Our thoughts and imagination are
the only real limits to our possibilities.

ORISON SWETT MARDEN

When my kids were little, they wanted to help me bake. It wasn't just that they were craving cake. They loved the process of working alongside me, cracking the eggs, pouring the oil, seeing the powdery cloud of flour when the mix is poured into the bowl, and taking turns stirring. In the end, there's the joy when you pull the pan out of the oven and find it's no longer a gloppy, runny mixture of raw ingredients, but a golden, spongy cake.

I think God lets us help Him cook. Let's face it—He doesn't need our assistance. He is perfectly capable of making decisions on His own, measuring out justice and mercy and grace. But when He asks us to pray, He's allowing us to be part of the process. It's probably a whole lot easier for Him when we're not bumbling around in the kitchen, spilling things, grabbing the wrong ingredients. But He does it for the delight on our faces when we see what comes out of the oven—when we see prayers answered and hearts healed and lives changed and love prevailing, when we know that even though we weren't necessary to the process, God still wanted us there, working right by His side.

Putting in the Effort

There's work to be done before an artist starts a painting. Choosing a subject, size, style, and medium; preparing a canvas; learning relevant techniques. Each of these sounds like a small thing, but, for example, an artist doesn't magically know how to mix paints to achieve the perfect shade or effect. He has to work on it until he becomes skilled—it doesn't necessarily come naturally. If he adds the wrong pigment to the mix, he'll end up with something closely resembling mud, not the clear, vibrant color he wants. That's why many artists experiment, especially when working with a new medium (watercolors, oils, pastels), creating charts documenting the hues created when this blue is mixed with that yellow, and so forth.

Do you remember the passage in Matthew 26, when Jesus went off to pray in the garden of Gethsemane? His disciples were busy, too—sleeping. Jesus was understandably angry. God expects us to bring a little something to the table. We can do all things through Him.[37] But in order for that to happen, a certain amount of "doing" is required on our part. We have to know Him and know how to get to Him.

I have friends who became Christians and immediately turned inward. They talk about their faith in reverent tones: "I'm in a time of preparation. God is strengthening me." Instead of going out and *doing*, they stay in and study. They associate only with other "strong" Christians. They read, pray, and spend hours contemplating the state of their souls.

None of these things are bad. In fact, I'd say they're all good, within reason. We need to spend time learning about God if we want to effectively serve and accurately represent Him. And there are times in

> *If the goal of an artist is to communicate, the goal of the Christian is to do the same. To communicate to God and about Him.*

all of our lives when we are particularly vulnerable, susceptible to ungodly influences, and we need a certain level of protection from that.

But if the goal of an artist is to communicate, the goal of the Christian is to do the same. To communicate *to* God and *about* Him. To do this, we have to talk to God ourselves and be out there among the people we want to reach. In the Gospel of Mark, Jesus tells the disciples, "Go into the world. Go everywhere and announce the Message of God's good news to one and all."[38]

No artist ever became great by cranking out an endless supply of color charts or gained acclaim for the quality of his nicely stretched canvases. We should absolutely learn the basics and then continue to delve deeper and deeper into our studies. But remember, the preparation—color charts, canvases, rows of neatly arranged tools—doesn't speak to people. It can't provoke emotion and solve problems. These exercises are part of our own growth, valuable to us as learning tools but not necessarily relevant to the person who views the painting hanging on the wall. We need to practice before we tackle the *real* work before us.

No matter how strongly you believe, even if your faith is an integral part of who you are, you won't always feel close to God. You may feel abandoned. The lack of noticeable answers may lead you to believe He's not listening, or He doesn't care, or He's not even there in the first place. You may struggle with finding the right words, or even if your words are plentiful, they may feel superficial and rote—nothing more than steps on the way to getting what you want.

No matter how much we'd like to believe otherwise, prayer is work. We want to keep it on a higher spiritual plane, separate from the drudgery of everyday chores. It's righteous and holy, so we must be better off for our part in it, right?

Yes. But at the same time, even though we are praying to a God who never changes—who is strong and steady and faithful and true—*even though*, I find myself unable to pray at times. I don't always see the benefits right away. I long for the days when I could spend hours face down in my living room, tears flowing, air crackling with intensity. The days before I was devastated by the loss of my mom. The times when there was no anger to work past, just this insatiable longing to find more of God. I've had those times, and I want them again.

Yet prayer isn't all about enjoying the bounty. Charlie, my friend Jen's husband, plants an impressive vegetable garden every year and loves reading seed catalogs and discussing the process in detail. As a family, they work hard to preserve the abundant harvest and give thanks for it all year long. Jen said, "I want to take pictures and write about it—enjoy the fruits of it—but I don't want to do the work! It's sweaty, it's dirty, and there are bugs out there."

Part of the value of prayer is in doing the work. Searching to find and fill the chinks in your own life as a result of seeing someone else's misfortune. Transforming judgment into empathy, and opening your eyes to the struggles of a particular person. Realizing that choices have consequences, and giving thanks for all the ways you've been shielded from more devastating outcomes. Recognizing that your strong marriage is vulnerable, too, and refocusing your attention on your spouse. Developing compassion for a man with a drug addiction and taking steps to turn from temptations that put all that matters to you at risk. Giving to someone in need and feeling grateful for the abundance you have to give.

Changes like these don't just happen like a light switch being flipped on. These understandings occur only through the process of prayer.

The Bible's authors repeatedly urge us to focus only on the day at hand. When God provided manna to the Israelites,[39] He gave them just enough food for that day—they couldn't store it up. What wasn't used *that day* went bad by the next morning. The Bible tells us that God's mercies are renewed daily.[40] That's why we have to pray daily.

Whether or not we think we have a gift for it.

Talent versus Desire

In Matt Appling's book *Life after Art*, he discusses how criticism of our art when we are children discourages many of us—for life.

> Eventually, most children come to believe that to create anything they have to be *creative*. They also come to believe

that creativity is a commodity, and they do not possess it. . . . It is as absurd as a gym in which only the athletic kids deserve to have fun. It is as absurd as a classroom in which only the smart kids deserve to learn to read or do math. It is as absurd as saying that only beautiful people deserve to fall in love and procreate, or that only rich people deserve to buy things, or that only religious people deserve to go to church.[41]

Matt claims, and I agree, that creating is more about the process than the result.

And nowhere is that more true than in prayer.

The Bible contains several lists of spiritual gifts and callings,[42] but God never limits who is allowed to pray. Not only that, but we're encouraged to "Pray in the Spirit at all times and on every occasion. Stay alert and be persistent in your prayers for all believers everywhere" (Ephesians 6:18).

It's easy to go along with the stereotypes you've been labeled with since your youth, saying you're a _____ (fill in the blank) instead of an artist. We try to preempt failure by simply removing ourselves from the game. But that same act prevents success, too. In a popular quotation attributed to Martha Graham, an influential American dancer and choreographer, she says, "Nobody cares if you can't dance well. Just get up and dance. Great dancers are not great because of their technique, they are great because of their passion."

I get it. It's why I nearly had an anxiety attack when I took my sixteen-year-old daughter to a daylong chemistry workshop at a nearby college. As I headed back to my car, the director of the program said, "Make sure you're back by 2:00. We're going to let the family do a lab while the students finish up. It'll be fun!"

I literally started to sweat. I was a good math student, and I could hold my own in English class. I did well in art and drafting. But chemistry? *Nightmare.* The thought of walking into a lab and having to figure out what to do to achieve the desired reaction? *Shudder.*

I wish I could tell you I conquered my fear and was waiting with excitement at 1:55 for the lab to begin. But I chickened out. I argued with myself all the way back to my car, finally settling on this: *I'm an adult, and I don't have to do something I don't want to do.*

So don't be me. On the other hand, one might argue that chemistry is not something I've used much in my twenty-five-year graphic design career. Prayer, though, is something we really can't afford to avoid.

Inspiration (Having Something to Say)

People talk about writer's block, but I think the equivalent thing happens even more often in prayer. You're ready to pray, but you don't know exactly what you want to say. My friend Gail sang in a choir most of her life and then took a three-year break. At that point, she realized that she *needed* to sing—something valuable was missing from her life—but she was scared to death. She wanted to be a soloist but admitted, "I had no idea what my voice sounded like. I'd spent the last twenty years trying to blend, to be part of a group."

Her fear went beyond that. In a choir, she explained, "All the guessing is taken out of it. They say 'Here's the music . . . rehearsal is at 4:00 . . . this is the key you're singing in.'" Her role was simply to show up and do what she was told. "But as a soloist, you can sing anything. Talk about intimidating."

It can be scary to start to pray in a new way, on your own, without someone directing you. But don't forget: Someone *will* be directing you. Try to listen for His voice. What that voice sounds like to you may be different than it sounds to me. In my life, when

I say that I've heard from God, I mean many different things. Sometimes His voice is like a strong, silent whisper inside my head—a flash, an instant knowingness, a revelation that is deeper and has more layers than I think I could have come up with on my own. His voice may show up in my writing, as I journal and discover conclusions that don't seem to be my own. I have never heard an audible voice, anything that someone sitting next to me would have also heard. But I've had friends offer unsolicited advice that directly answers questions I just asked in prayer. One day I had lunch with Peggy and asked her a question I'd kept to myself for years, always afraid to ask. When I got home and checked my e-mail, there was a video link in an e-mail from a well-known pastor whose newsletter I had just subscribed to days before. It just so happened to be a direct answer to this question that I had never seen or heard discussed before.

At times, as I pray about a decision, it feels as though one option gently floats to the surface, like a bubble, and rests there. It's not loud or momentous. It's as though other choices recede, leaving one in front of me. When you seek God, ask for His involvement, and pray with a sincere desire to hear from Him; you can trust that the answer that rises to the top—if it doesn't conflict with your knowledge of the character and will of God—is from Him. You just know.

Making Time for Your Craft

When my kids were little, I would set a kitchen timer ten minutes before their bedtime, letting them know that the day was drawing to a close. It was time to slow down, find a bedtime story, pick up their toys (or not). When the timer started ticking, it gave them due notice that it was time to shut down for the night.

Scripture encourages us to pray in the morning, to start our days by offering ourselves to God and praising Him for who He is. I am so not a morning person, and I confess I've never managed a regular morning quiet time. I pray in the shower and—when I remember—offer prayers before I roll out of bed. But I don't get up early, although I know many people who have their best times with God then. I tend to be able to still my mind better during the afternoon, when the kids are at school and the morning work crises have been averted, or late at night, when the house is silent.

> *Prayer is something you can hold on to for the rest of your days, a foundation on which you can build everything else.*

If you can discipline yourself to have a regular quiet time, it's a wonderful thing, because it will signal your mind—and your soul—that it's time to focus. Many artists and writers insist that establishing a routine is a key condition for creativity. I can't disagree with that, but don't let your ritual replace spontaneous prayer throughout the day. Be open and willing to watch for and respond to those nudges, those times when something in your spirit prompts you to pray. Stay open to the ways God might steer you. And when you feel that nudge, allow yourself to pause. To open your heart—and mind— in that moment.

Acceptance

It is particularly hard for most artists to accept a result that is not extraordinary. We have trouble believing that what we've done is good, or even good enough.

It is, though.

If you sit down (or stand up, or kneel, or hold your arms to the sky, or lie facedown on the carpet) to pray, consider that a success. If you talk to God while you stir the soup or drive the car, acknowledge that you took a step in the right direction. It's not complicated: Are you praying? If yes, stop criticizing yourself. If no, well, then start. I'm not making light of the very real emotional and situational stumbling blocks that keep us from praying, make us afraid to begin, or get in the way of what we're asking. I'm simply saying that in the realm of prayer, there is no room for shame. As long as you are praying, you are doing the right thing. What you've done (or haven't done) before is a lot less important than what you are doing right now.

Remember, though, prayer is not something you can check off your to-do list. You never completely finish. It's ongoing, or should be—the more you pray, the more you will be changed. It doesn't matter whether you pray upside down or in a more traditional way. Whether you read the Bible or listen to worship music. What matters is that you keep doing it.

The apostle Paul tells us to "Never stop praying."[43] Through different phases of life, your approach will vary. As circumstances change, as people come into and go out of your life, your emotions and motivations will evolve. Your insights will change. Your intensity will wax and wane. Your beliefs and convictions will evolve. But prayer is something you can hold on to for the rest of your days, a foundation on which you can build everything else. You may pick up bits and pieces here and there. You'll have different influences, various inspiration, assorted hurdles. Your prayer life will not be like anyone else's. Your style will be unique to you.

It's time to get to work. Your blank canvas awaits.

PRAYER PALETTE

OVERCOMING YOUR LACK. Consider the subheads in this chapter (putting in the effort, talent versus desire, inspiration, making time for your craft, and acceptance). In which area do you feel the least equipped? Ask God in prayer to help you find practical ways to overcome this and make a list of steps you can take. You already have what you need to do so—you only need God to provide the confidence that you are missing.

Looking up at one of the most famous paintings in the world

CHAPTER 22

LOOKING TO THE MASTERS

(LEARNING FROM THE EXPERTS)

Come near to the holy men and women of the past and you will soon feel the heat of their desire after God. They mourned for Him, they prayed and wrestled and sought for Him day and night in season and out, and when they had found Him the finding was all the sweeter for the long seeking.

A. W. TOZER, *THE PURSUIT OF GOD*

When I started attending my church, I was fascinated—and a little disturbed—by the way people prayed. Many services ended with people kneeling or lying before the altar, laying hands on others as they prayed, speaking in tongues, dancing in worship. I found myself forgetting that I was supposed to be praying because I was so busy watching. What are they doing? *Why?* I understood that the way they prayed and worshiped was different than the way a Catholic, Baptist, or Presbyterian might worship, but I also knew that, whether I ever joined them or not in this practice (I did), I could learn a lot by paying attention. Trying what they were trying. Asking questions. Watching.

In the Renaissance and throughout history, artists weren't suddenly "discovered" and made famous. There was no *European Artist Idol* to audition for—just a long road lined with hard work. Nearly all of the men labeled as great masters began as humble apprentices, often beginning with tasks that had little to do with art. They would sweep floors, prepare panels for painting, and learn to grind and mix pigments to make paint. Eventually, the apprentice would assist his master by completing smaller, lesser tasks—sketching, copying existing paintings, casting sculptures. When his skills had sufficiently developed and he had proven himself capable, he might graduate to the task of painting the background before the master tackled the main subjects. If a student showed extraordinary skill, he would eventually become a master himself, opening up his own workshop and selecting apprentices of his own. But through it all, the artist never forgot or neglected the steps he learned along the way.

Twyla Tharp sees that kind of mastery evident in other professions, too. In *The Creative Habit*, she writes:

> Leonardo [da Vinci] understood that the better you know
> the nuts and bolts of your craft, the more fully you can
> express your talents.

The great painters are incomparable draftsmen. They also know how to mix their own paint, grind it, put in the fixative; no task is too small to be worthy of their attention.

The great composers are usually dazzling musicians. They have to know their instrument before they can make it sing the tune in their head. . . .

A great chef can chop and dice better than anyone in the kitchen.

The best fashion designers are invariably virtuosos with a needle and thread . . . they still know how to cut and sew better than anyone else working for them.

The best writers are well-read people. They have the richest appreciation of words, the biggest vocabularies, the keenest ear for language. They also know their grammar. Words and language are their tools, and they have learned how to use them. . . .

What all these people have in common is that they have mastered the underlying skills of their creative domain, and built their creativity on the solid foundation of those skills.[44]

No matter what you're doing, observation is a valuable method of learning—working side by side with the experts, imitating their actions and copying their motions until you are able to do the work without help. The process of doing teaches you to take what works, discard what doesn't, and make the process your own through adaptation and application.

Jeff Bullas, an influential blogger, mentor, coach, and speaker, writes, "Your job as an artist, producer, creator and author is to shamelessly start stealing. Many people of perceived genius and as front runners in their industry have perfected the art of stealing. All creative work stands on what has gone before."[45] I agree, but since the Bible tells us repeatedly that we should not steal, let's use less inflammatory words—such as *borrow. Learn. Watch. Be inspired.*

The key is to understand that merely watching is not always enough to create a lasting impact. My friend Elizabeth teaches art, and one day she showed a boy how to make a scratchboard. Step-by-step, they did it together. The next week, when he came in, she asked him to sit down and make another one on his own. He was stumped and had no idea where to start. He'd only done it once before, and he hadn't paid much attention because she was essentially doing it for him.

Her story reminds me of the disciples who sat at the feet of Jesus. They followed Him, watched Him, and listened to Him. They shared dinner with Him, waited for Him to pray, and took a frightening boat ride while He was napping as peacefully as a baby. Even though they were right there with Him, able to reach out and touch His physical body, they still didn't understand everything He said. There's a lot they missed (which I find comforting, because if they couldn't figure it all out and they were *right there with Him*, it's okay that I don't always get it either). At least they consistently addressed Him as "Teacher," showing they understood that He had specific knowledge and revelatory understanding— things they wanted to learn.

In a way, I think the disciples failed to notice many opportunities because of their lack of understanding. God was right in front of them, and they still sometimes didn't *see* Him. In some of the stories, their replies seem purposely obtuse. In their defense, though, no one had ever seen anyone like Jesus before. No person had ever had such intimate knowledge of the Divine. In effect, the disciples were apprentices. After Jesus was crucified and resurrected, they finally understood the full reality of what they had seen. So they used their knowledge to train others.

In matters of spiritual growth, as in art, one of the best ways to learn is by observing someone who has been doing it for a while. It's one thing to bow your head, maybe even raise your hands in the middle of a church service during the swelling chorus of your favorite song, alongside a hundred other people. But it's another to do it when you're on your own, alone in a quiet room. Self-consciousness sets in (*I feel silly. I bet I look ridiculous*). Words, which spill out

> *In matters of spiritual growth, as in art, one of the best ways to learn is by watching someone who has been doing it for a while.*

of your mouth at the coffee shop with your best friend, come slowly, hesitantly. And then doubt (*Is He really listening? Does He really care what I have to say?*).

But if you practice—if you make it a habit to implement the activities of other people of faith, such as spending time with God, meditating on who He is, talking to Him about your joys and quandaries and frustrations—it gets easier. You may no longer need to rely on someone else's words, on rote repetition. You may spend longer times praying, longer than you ever imagined, just sitting in His presence. Talking. Listening. You may yearn for more time. What started out as something awkward—a list of instructions for an unfamiliar process—will become natural. And before long, you'll feel a fundamental shift. Because practice shows. Prayer transforms attitudes and smooths rough edges. Your friends will see the change. But even if they don't, even if nobody knows but you and God, it still matters. Jesus promises rewards for those who pray in private.[46] The rewards aren't always tangible. You can't always measure them. No ROI charts, no promises. But you will *feel* the difference. You will know. And you will hold those times close to your heart, because there is nothing—*nothing*—like burrowing in with the Father.

And now, dear brothers and sisters, one final thing. Fix
your thoughts on what is true, and honorable, and right,
and pure, and lovely, and admirable. Think about things
that are excellent and worthy of praise.

PHILIPPIANS 4:8

In college, I took a life drawing class. The human body is a
work of art. (If you're uncomfortable with the idea, keep in mind
that the models don't mind disrobing to make a little money. It's
not sleazy. It's art.) The models know how valuable it is to an artist
to observe and draw from real life.

We had one particular model whom I hated to draw. He was
really, really tall, with unusually long legs. He wasn't unattractive,
but his body had an awkward shape. I was troubled by how much
I disliked drawing him, until it came to me: This was art. Realism.
We had to draw as accurately as possible. No matter how well I
drew him, the drawing still looked awkward.

In spite of that, the act of drawing this man was valuable. In
fact, it probably taught me more than it would have if he had a
perfect, Roman sculpture-worthy bod. Had his frame been more
ideally proportioned, I would have relied on my preconceived
ideas of how he *should* look. I wouldn't have had to observe as
closely, and I would have leaned more on my intellect than on
actual observation.

I wanted to blame my poor drawings on this man's flaws, but
really, the length of his legs had very little to do with the sub-
standard quality of my sketches. Sometimes we refuse to accept
responsibility for our involvement in a less-than-ideal situation.
But it's a crutch when we use one person's failing as an excuse to
keep from trying.

I have friends who are Christians but who don't want to be
identified as such because of the poor impressions other Christians

have made. In some cases, it goes beyond poor impressions into atrocious, ungodly behavior. You've seen them on the news, shouting hateful words to someone who is different than they are, or someone who has the gall to hold a different set of beliefs. They feel justified in attacking, in forcing their own views on everyone else. I know others who do *not* believe in God but who, like an artist, observe carefully what they see as a way to make sense of the world.

When people—both Christians and non-Christians—see ungodly attitudes and acts among those who profess to be Christian, they turn away from Christianity. The appeal of a life revolving around faith is lost to them because they don't ever see the redeeming side of it. What they see doesn't look like Christ. They witness hypocrisy and petty feuds within churches. They're excluded for loving the wrong person or for committing a sin that carries a public consequence. The teenage couple having sex might be overlooked—until the girl turns up pregnant and then all of a sudden finds herself condemned and pushed away. In our society, appearance seems to matter more to most folks than values and actions. (Brings to mind the Pharisees, come to think of it.)

The Christian church doesn't always do such a great job with public relations. But when a friend uses the argument that if this is what Christianity is, she wants no part of it, something in me rises up. I get it. I really do. If this is what Christianity is, I don't want to be part of it, either. But that argument is flawed. I don't believe that those behaviors—those tragedies and injustices and just plain mean people—*are* Christianity. It doesn't look like Jesus or act like Jesus. So it must not represent Jesus.

As Christians, we have no business participating in atrocious, hurtful behaviors, no matter how "Christian" the others involved say they are. It is up to us to raise the standard, to model the truth, reflect God's love, and show compassion. We are to extend our hands to draw people close, not to push them away. We are to find what is true and noble and right[47] and dwell on it. We're called to live it. If enough of us do this, if we do the best we can, while all the time keeping our eyes fixed on God, the world will see a change.

I, for one, want to see God in all His magnificence. And in humility, I want to let Him shine through me. I want His light to illuminate a dark moment for someone I am with. I want to try to demonstrate the things that *are* of God. And it is my prayer that the people I meet who are on the fence, who wonder if perhaps there is some truth to this Christian life, something noble or admirable, will notice the parts I got right. And ignore the ones with no resemblance to the ideal. I want to tell them that they—that all of us—can learn from anyone. Even if that person is less than perfect.

Persevere, and sort through what you see. Ask God to show you where He is in anything you witness, study, or participate in. Don't limit your field of view to religious figures. Inspiration—creative and spiritual—is everywhere.

> *Ask God to show you where He is in anything you witness, study, or participate in. Inspiration—creative and spiritual—is everywhere.*

Going back to my early days at my church—when I would sit at the altar trying not to be fazed by the type of worship and prayer all around me—what kept me there, what had me riveted, was my absolute conviction that it was real. The people were genuine. I watched and watched as people spoke in tongues, trying to decide if they were faking it, wondering if they were dancing because they were weird or wanted to fit in or because they really felt the Spirit.

One beautiful aspect of my church is that people regularly stand up and talk about how they see God in the middle of their illnesses, job losses, addictions, or money troubles. Whether they're lonely and looking for a spouse, devastated (or thrilled) to be divorced, or tossed about by the cares of this world, they share where they are. Much like Colleese (chapter 14), who sings to God about where she is at the moment, these people offer all they have. They explain how they see and feel and hear Him. How God has restored what they lost. Healed what was broken. Made something great out of nothing.

What I know to be true about God I know because people showed me. Not by pointing out a Scripture, not by singing well at church or holding up their hands as they prayed, not because I saw a big billboard telling me to believe or I'll go to hell. I know what I know because I've watched people endure. It's easy to proclaim that God is good when you received the promotion you wanted, your marriage is solid, the tumor is benign, and there's money in the bank. But it's powerful to see someone profess his or her belief in God's goodness when outside circumstances aren't good.

I have felt compassion for them—and from them. I have been treated with consideration. I have witnessed people giving self-lessly and without reservation, and I have seen their peace even during times of turmoil. I've witnessed reconciliation and hope. It is true what the Bible says: "Blessed are those who believe without seeing me" (John 20:29). I want that kind of faith. And I can have it, because even though I have not seen God face-to-face, I *have* seen Him. I've seen His signature all over the scenes He's painted, both in and out of my life. And all that I've seen has helped me to believe.

When you observe others, you don't have to adopt all of their actions or beliefs. Take in the parts that work for you. Reserve judgment—but use wisdom—as you watch. If you remain open and ask God to reveal, you will find inspiration everywhere, in every activity, event, situation, or person. Because that's where God is. Everywhere.

PRAYER PALETTE

This world is but a canvas to our imagination.
~HENRY DAVID THOREAU

LOOKING FOR INSPIRATION. Even among master artists, styles and techniques vary. Van Gogh's turbulent, swirling strokes are very different from Matisse's decorative shapes. Yet both had a dramatic impact on the world of art.

To learn how to pray, there are plenty of places to turn. If you are a Christian, the Bible provides no better source of inspiration than Jesus—but there's also plenty to learn from others. Artists can inspire us spiritually, and spiritual leaders may inspire us creatively. Listen to music and read books. Learn from pastors, speakers, teachers, and friends whose faith illuminates each day. Look around, but don't limit yourself to looking within the walls of the church. Watch how the waiter treats his customers. See how the lady next door volunteers to serve Thanksgiving dinner at a shelter. Notice the teacher whose words of encouragement convince a student to stop cutting herself.

Let learning and exploring be another form of your prayer. And don't ever stop looking. Because that's where you will find God. Everywhere. Inside. Outside. In the dark, in the light. Hidden and in plain sight. Backwards and forwards.

Even—most especially—upside down.

Are you ready to see things differently now?

CHAPTER 23

A PERMANENT PERSPECTIVE

Like other global skills—for example, reading, driving, skiing, and walking—drawing is made up of component skills that become integrated into a whole skill. Once you have learned ... them, you can draw. ... Progress takes the form of practice, refinement of technique, and learning what to use the skills for.

BETTY EDWARDS, *DRAWING ON THE RIGHT SIDE OF THE BRAIN*

253

When I first taught a Bible study about praying upside down, I wanted to demonstrate the differences between the right-side-up and upside-down drawings. I practiced at home that afternoon, looking at the drawings with disappointment. They looked more or less the same. Maybe I should try drawing a different image? I found another and tried again.

Then I understood. Once you learn to see in a different way, you can't go back. My whole life, I'd been learning to see. I'd learned about shapes, line, contrast, and values. I already knew to see past what I *expected* to see and observe what was *actually* in front of me.

At the same time, my drawings weren't all that great. Because knowing it and doing it are two different things. King David's mighty men trained until they could shoot arrows or sling stones equally well with their left hand or right so that they could protect themselves from any direction. One session of practice would not be enough. We need to do more than know it in our heads—we need to use our skills day after day.

I was definitely out of practice. Oh, I knew the process. I looked at the negative space between objects and tried to use those to define what *was* there. I measured real distances and tried to keep them proportionate. I looked at where the lines met the edges of the border and noticed the places where the lines subtly curved, doing my best not to let my mind label the shapes as objects or define them. But, still, it was hard to take what I saw and convert that into hand movements that would produce the result I wanted. The shapes I put on the paper were distorted and didn't match what I saw.

During those years after Mom's cancer diagnosis, I knew my relationship with God was at a critical point. I knew I needed to pray. I knew that time spent alone with God would heal the hurting places. But when I sat down, it didn't work that way. I knew what to do but had trouble doing it. I knew how I was supposed to pray, yet the words wouldn't come. I'd try to listen for Him, but instead my mind would wander to the grocery list and projects I needed to complete that day. The less I prayed, the more out of practice I became. And the farther I felt from God. Losing Mom was the biggest struggle I've ever faced, but there have been plenty of others. Rejection. Money. Work failures. Relationships falling apart. Health issues. And since losses seem to compound as we get older, I know I'll have many more.

I am fortunate because I have had intimate times with God. I've had a vibrant prayer life, one in which He's revealed things to me, talked to me, and wooed me. Those times with God were emotional, reverent, energizing, humbling, renewing. So even though I was out of practice and I hadn't felt those things for a while, I knew it was worth the effort to work my way back to Him. Of course, He had never left me, but because I stopped recognizing Him, it felt as though I had to find Him all over again.

> *Even in the lowest times, God's still there showing me truths. He never condemns. He doesn't want my disappointment in myself to keep me away.*

But here's the truly amazing thing: *He let me.*

I have my good days and bad ones. I have weeks of riding on a spiritual high, and several days at a time when I spiral downward. Even in the lowest times, though, I've come to understand that I can still see Him. He's still there showing me truths. He still answers the little prayers I shoot up, under my breath, almost before I'm aware that I'm doing it. He never condemns. He doesn't want my disappointment in myself to keep me away.

And so I keep trying. I practice a little every day. When I feel stuck, I try something new. When I'm out of ideas, I watch someone else or pick up a new book or flip through the Bible. I read devotionals and listen to songs written about Him and discipline myself to pray the second I read or hear a prayer request. When I can't sleep, I try to remember them all, and I lift them up, silently, to Him, almost like counting sheep. In the morning, I don't beat myself up for falling asleep before I was finished. I shake it off and pick up where I left off.

I am the biggest hurdle I will ever face in my faith.

God doesn't require variety or originality from us. We're the ones who put expectations onto prayer and our ability to perform it. In His sweetness, God has shown me that I needed to broaden my definition of prayer. He welcomes my prayers, however I pray. He accepts my offerings, whether I'm offering my housecleaning as prayer or meditating on liturgy or writing page after page in my journal. I'm the one who needs the variety. It's how I overcome my short attention span. It's how I rekindle my desire for Him.

In art, to branch out, you might try drawing with your left hand instead of your right. Use paint instead of pastels. Create a mural instead of a miniature. In the realm of the divine, there are no limits to the ways we can touch God. These upside-down prayer techniques are just a start. We often need a change of scenery in order to see something new, unexpected, or inspiring. To look at God from a new perspective—permanently. He never tires of surprising us, and He never stops creating. He never stops speaking. He never ceases to love us. He never gives up, and He never walks away. He is always there, always wanting to reveal who He is, eternally offering us more. More, more, more.

If you'll just open your eyes to see Him.

Acknowledgments

And these God-chosen lives all around—what
splendid friends they make!
PSALM 16:3, *The Message*

No matter how you look at it—inside out or upside down—I couldn't have done this alone. My friends have been the best part of this journey, especially those I wrote about in the heart of this book. You'll always be in mine. And special thanks to Sharon Rapoport, Julie Baird, Kathryn Schueren, and Suzanne Thompson for helping me keep sane.

Peggy Miller, I watched one day as you bowed your head, holding your hands in front of you. You've shown me, again and again, that when you offer your hands to Jesus, He grabs hold and doesn't let go. You're the best kind of friend.

Nathan Miller, I couldn't ask for a better pastor, teacher, and friend. I see in your eyes the same sparkle that Jesus must have had in His.

To my church, Grace & Mercy Ministries, I only know what I know because you've let me into your lives and wrapped your arms around me tight. You're my inspiration.

I'm grateful to all of my early readers, whose suggestions made this book better: Jodi Barnes, Alison Bliss, Terri DeVries, Irene

Fridsma, Sarah Schmitt, Marcia Kendall, and Kerry Dunham. And to the earliest of my early readers, Lisa Rice Wheeler, the one who believed in me long, long before I believed in myself: I don't know what I'd do without you!

Writing wouldn't be nearly as fun without the Cool Kids (Joe Roper, Sarah Schmitt, Terri DeVries, Irene Fridsma, Dan Johnson, Kelsey Timmerman, Lisa Wheeler, and Julie Hyzy), who have shown me that every girl needs her very own fan club. Jama Kehoe Bigger and the Midwest Writers Workshop deserve the credit for most of what I know about writing.

"Writing a book" is such an abstract proposition—until some really amazing people step in and do their thing. People like Blythe Daniel, my agent, who wasn't afraid to look at things upside down. Sarah Atkinson, associate acquisitions director for Tyndale Momentum, who took a chance on this first-time author. Bonne Steffen, editor extraordinaire, who pulled far better words from me than I knew I had. And all the others at Tyndale House Publishers who are so encouraging, lovely, and extraordinarily good at what they do. In other words, every single person there.

My favorite time of day is that pre-dinner hour I spend with Kerry and Doug Dunham. I admire Doug's always-thoughtful perspective on life. I love that I don't have to hug my sissy for her to know how much I love her and that I only have to walk across the driveway to borrow a can of chicken broth.

I could never express to my dad, Rob O'Dell, how amazing he is or how much I love him, so I can only hope this book shows him.

I'm overwhelmed with gratitude for my husband, Tim, for always believing in me. Always, without fail. No matter how busy I get, how cranky I am, or how crazy my plan.

I'm overflowing with love for my kids—Katie, my mini-me who surprises me over and over by appearing to be proud of that fact; Anna, an amazing girl who gives the best hugs and notices the things I notice; and Bobby, who has challenged my mind and creativity every day of his life. For that I am so glad.

And, of course, I'm here only because of the One who creates all things, holds all things, and reveals all things. This—and all that I do—is for You.

More about the Images

 Introduction: This drawing by Pablo Picasso—*Portrait of Igor Stravinsky*—(turned upside down) was used by art teacher Betty Edwards in her now famous experiment. Her research became the basis for the 1979 book *Drawing on the Right Side of the Brain*. The original 1920 drawing (right-side up) of the famed Russian composer is at the Musée Picasso in Paris.

 Chapter 1: Having two houses at one time taught me what to hold on to and what to let go of—and how much easier it was to let God carry the worries instead of trying to do it myself. Illustration copyright © art4all /Shutterstock.

 Chapter 2: All I wanted was to see a "Sold" sign in front of my old house. I just didn't realize I'd have to look upside down in order to see it. Photograph copyright © Kelly O'Dell Stanley.

 Chapter 3: The statue (on the left) is a replica of the sculptured image created in 1607 by Marc'Antonio Prestinari of St. Agapito and is located on the south side of the Milan Cathedral (Duomo di Milano) in Italy. The original sculpture can be seen inside the Duomo Museum, where it was moved for preservation. Photograph copyright © Claudio Giovanni Colombo/ Shutterstock.

Chapter 4: Even at age four, I was trying to steal the limelight when Gaildene Hamilton, a reporter for the *Crawfordsville Journal Review*, came to interview my dad, Rob O'Dell. One thing I never outgrew? Being proud to belong to him. Photo from author's personal collection.

Chapter 5: This watercolor, *Cornstalk Creek*, is named after the place that inspired it. Rob O'Dell paints the everyday scenery he sees around him in Indiana. Watercolor copyright © Rob O'Dell.

Chapter 6: What do you see? Look again, focusing only on the white, or looking exclusively at the black. There are often two ways to look at one image, as Edgar Rubin, a Danish psychologist, showed us when he developed the original illusion around 1915. Illustration copyright © pio3/Shutterstock.

Chapter 7: Jonas Ghionzoli and his mother, Jennifer, illustrate how point of view is determined by where you are and what you see. Photograph copyright © Tyndale House Publishers, Inc.

Chapter 8: *Showing Her Age*, a watercolor by Rob O'Dell, illustrates his use of negative space. The barn's roof is not actually painted, nor is the snow on the ground. Instead, details like the birds perching where the roofline should be give the illusion of something more. Watercolor copyright © Rob O'Dell.

Chapter 9: In this sketch by Elizabeth Lincourt, we see that the basic human form is made up of simple geometric shapes. Blocking in an image in this way helps an artist understand what lies beneath the surface, helping her draw a more accurate likeness. Sketch copyright © Elizabeth Lincourt. Used with permission.

Chapter 10: In this photo of railroad tracks that I took near my hometown in rural Indiana, all lines point to the horizon. Using the idea of perspective can teach us a lot about faith as well as art. Photograph copyright © Kelly O'Dell Stanley.

Chapter 11: Using the grid method allows an artist to accurately copy an image by assuring accurate placement of shapes along the lines of the grid as demonstrated by Elizabeth Lincourt. Photograph and sketch copyright © Elizabeth Lincourt. Used with permission.

Chapter 12: Although both have value, there's a substantial difference between Rob O'Dell's sketch of a door and the finished watercolor. The sketch is a valuable tool to quickly lay out the basic information, but the painting provides additional detail and expression. Sketch copyright © Rob O'Dell.

Chapter 13: A sketchbook captures the exploration and thought process of the artist—in this case, my exploration of different logo directions for the Midwest Writers Workshop. You can see that I used regular pencils, colored pencils, and cut-and-pasted images found online to capture my ideas. To see the final logo, visit http://www.midwestwriters.org/. Photography copyright © Kelly O'Dell Stanley.

Chapter 14: In this Egyptian papyrus, the size of the figures is based upon their relative importance and status within the culture. Hieratic scale isn't exclusive to Egyptian art; playing with the size of objects in proportion to other objects can be a way to emphasize them. Photograph copyright © Krikkiat/Shutterstock.

Chapter 15: Artist Koko Toyama admits that it takes time and practice to train yourself not to look at what you're drawing as you're doing it. In this contour drawing of a woman, she was copying the woman from a photograph. Illustration copyright © Tyndale House Publishers, Inc.

Chapter 16: After we'd done all the work to accessorize Lola, the four of us posed with our showgirl. From left to right: Peggy Miller, me, Tami Sells, and Glenna Florence. Photograph copyright © Kelly O'Dell Stanley.

Chapter 17: When you enlarge a printed photo, you'll see that the image is made up of dots of different sizes and colors. From a distance, though, the brain converts the dots into one continuous image, as shown in this eye illustration copyright © Ilter Alkan/Shutterstock. This technique of using smaller individual components to create a larger whole image sometimes incorporates surprising items—such as Joel Brochu's piece, at http://www.inspirefusion.com/beagle-sprinkles-portrait/.

Chapter 18: With just circles and lines, faces showing a range of emotions emerge. Whether you are a fan of this emoticon-type of communication or not, there is no question it has become a universal language. Illustration copyright © yod67/Shutterstock.

Chapter 19: Photographer Stephen Vosloo intentionally used a long exposure in order to achieve a sense of stillness in his image—*Early Dawn*—of Lake Michigan. By removing the distractions of reflections and waves in the water, it evokes serenity and simplicity, gently drawing the eyes of the viewer to the main focal point. Photograph copyright © Stephen Vosloo.

Chapter 20: Since different tools produce contrasting results, an artist will keep a variety of implements within easy reach. These are a few my dad keeps by his right hand. Photograph copyright © Kelly O'Dell Stanley.

Chapter 21: Artists develop distinctive personal styles, as shown in this portrait collage pulled together from the work of seven different people. Art pieces (l. to r. from top left to bottom right) copyright © Hannah Hawkins, copyright © Liliya Kulianionak/Shutterstock, copyright © Natasha R. Graham/Shutterstock, copyright © Boyan Dimitrov/Shutterstock, copyright © siloto/Shutterstock, copyright © Rybkina2009/Shutterstock, copyright © Liliya Kulianionak/Shutterstock, copyright © DeepGreen/Shutterstock.

Chapter 22: *The Creation of Adam*, one of the nine stories from the book of Genesis frescoed on the Vatican's Sistine Chapel ceiling, painted by Michelangelo between 1508 and 1512. Photograph copyright © cynoclub/Shutterstock.

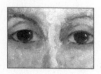

Chapter 23: God is present and active all around. We just have to keep our eyes open in order to see the countless ways He shows Himself to us. Detail from painting copyright © Sandra Lee Baron.

Additional credits for interior art used throughout the book: Watercolor background detail copyright © luceluceluce/Dollarphotoclub; photograph of frame copyright © Boggy/Dollarphotoclub; illustration of painter's palette copyright © art-romashka/Shutterstock. All rights reserved by each copyright holder on all images used.

Notes

1. To anoint something means to pour or smear oil on it to designate that the object or person is set apart for divine purposes. Originally used in the Old Testament to consecrate kings and priests, the practice is mentioned numerous times in the New Testament. James 5:14 says, "You should call for the elders of the church to come and pray over you, anointing you with oil in the name of the Lord." The oil itself is not magical. It's merely a way to designate an object as holy.
2. Mark 9:24
3. Charles Solomon, "Future Style," *Los Angeles Times*, October 21, 1986.
4. Exodus 16
5. A concordance is a book that provides definitions, locations, related words, and translations for the original Hebrew and Greek words used in the Bible. It's a tool that allows the reader to find words with similar meanings, explore context, and find other mentions of the same words.
6. 1 John 1:9
7. All names in this story have been changed.
8. Ephesians 6:16: "Hold up the shield of faith to stop the fiery arrows of the devil."
9. Romans 8:26-27
10. 2 Samuel 11
11. 1 Samuel 17
12. Psalm 63, among others
13. John 14:3
14. Hebrews 13:8
15. Philippians 4:6
16. Matthew 6:8
17. Matthew 7:24-27
18. Steven Aguilera, "What Perspective Really Means in Drawing and Art" (ezine article), September 16, 2009, http://ezinearticles.com/?What-Perspective-Really -Means-in-Drawing-and-Art&id=2931257.

19. Ecclesiastes 3:1-8
20. Heather Patterson, "Perspective {revisited}," *Come What May and Love It* (blog), September 23, 2013, http://comewhatmayandloveit.com/perspective-revisited-2/.
21. Stephen Rodrick, "McEnroe a role model? You cannot be serious!" *The Australian*, August 27, 2011, http://www.theaustralian.com.au/news/features/mcenroe-a-role -model-you-cannot-be-serious/story-e6frg8h6-1226122110149?nk=052ded753e9 40c11ccb15cea25969bbd.
22. Kristen Levithan, "Mother-Writer: Toni Morrison," *Motherese* (blog), August 28, 2013, http://mothereseblog.com/2013/08/28/mother-writer-toni-morrison/.
23. Kenneth Clark, *Leonardo da Vinci* (London: Penguin Books, 1989).
24. Follow security guidelines for sufficiently strong passwords. These are just examples.
25. Hebrews 4:12
26. Exodus 14:15-18
27. Psalm 23:4
28. Addie Zierman, "Intercessory Prayer: Doubt and Faith and Amy," *How to Talk Evangelical* (blog), June 12, 2012, http://addiezierman.com/2012/06/12 /intercessory-prayer-doubt-and-faith-and-amy/.
29. Frank Norris, *The Responsibilities of the Novelist* (Doubleday, Page & Company, 1903), 241–242.
30. Matthew 3:12
31. John 3:19-21
32. Matthew 6:1-4
33. Anne Lamott, *Help, Thanks, Wow* (New York: Penguin, 2012).
34. Napoleon Hill, *Think and Grow Rich* (New York: Penguin, 2005), 139.
35. Deuteronomy 31:6, NIV
36. Jon Acuff, "The 9 Words You Missed." See https://www.goodreads.com /author_blog_posts/4159372-the-9-words-you-missed.
37. Philippians 4:13
38. Mark 16:15, *The Message*
39. Exodus 16
40. Lamentations 3:22-23
41. Matt Appling, *Life after Art* (Chicago: Moody Publishers, 2013), 37.
42. Romans 12:6-8; 1 Corinthians 12:8-10; 1 Corinthians 12:28; Ephesians 4:11; 1 Peter 4:11
43. 1 Thessalonians 5:17
44. Twyla Tharp, *The Creative Habit* (New York: Simon & Schuster, 2006), 162–163.
45. Jeff Bullas, "Why You Should Steal Content," *Jeffbullas.com* (blog), February 12, 2013, http://www.jeffbullas.com/2013/02/13/why-you-should-steal-content/.
46. Matthew 6:6
47. Philippians 4:8

About the Author

Kelly O'Dell Stanley is a graphic designer and writer. This book is the junction of all of her passions—faith, art, and writing. With more than two decades of experience in advertising, three kids ranging from teens to young adult, and a husband of more than two decades, she's learned to look at life in unconventional ways—sometimes even upside down.

A regular monthly contributor to Internet Café Devotions, Kelly's work has appeared in several publications, and her awards include first place in Inspirational Writing in the 2013 *Writer's Digest* Competition. Her design work has been included in design anthologies and in *PRINT Magazine*'s Design Annual, and she's received design awards from the NAHB, Public Relations Society of America, the Webby Competition, and Art Directors Club of Indiana.

Kelly lives in Crawfordsville, Indiana, where she has lunch with friends, coffee with her iPad, and spends any otherwise-unscheduled evenings on the couch with her husband—though those evenings don't come as often as she'd like. She is full of doubt and full of faith, constantly seeking new ways to see what's happening all around her.

You may connect with her on her blog, www.prayingup sidedown.com, on Facebook (Kelly O'Dell Stanley, author), or on Twitter (@kellyostanley).

*For resources to help you pray
upside down, including exclusive video
content and downloads, visit*
www.PrayingUpsideDownBook.com.

**Includes an 8-week study guide for
small groups or individual use**

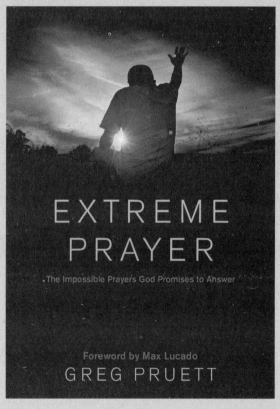